MR. HORACE DINSMORE SR.

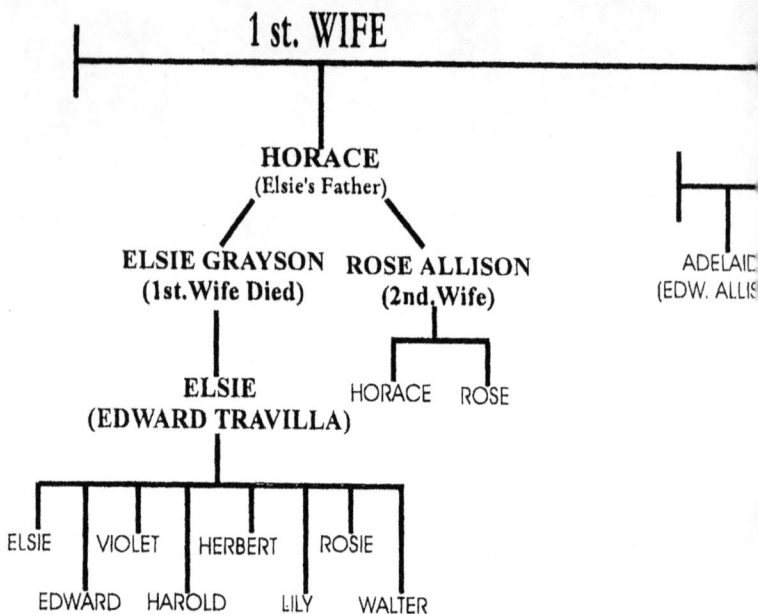

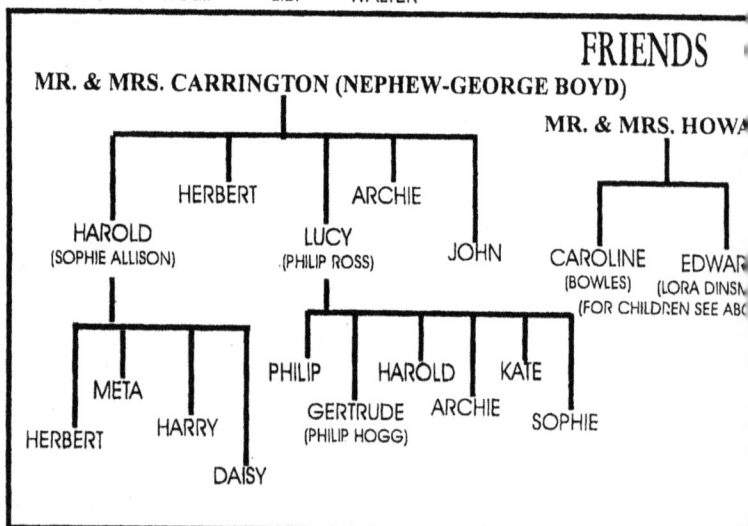

1 st. WIFE

HORACE
(Elsie's Father)

ELSIE GRAYSON
(1st.Wife Died)

ROSE ALLISON
(2nd.Wife)

ADELAID
(EDW. ALLIS

ELSIE
(EDWARD TRAVILLA)

HORACE   ROSE

ELSIE   VIOLET   HERBERT   ROSIE

EDWARD   HAROLD   LILY   WALTER

FRIENDS

MR. & MRS. CARRINGTON (NEPHEW-GEORGE BOYD)

MR. & MRS. HOWA

HERBERT   ARCHIE

HAROLD
(SOPHIE ALLISON)

LUCY
(PHILIP ROSS)

JOHN

CAROLINE
(BOWLES)
(FOR CHILDREN SEE AB

EDWAR
(LORA DINSN

META

HERBERT   HARRY

DAISY

PHILIP   HAROLD   KATE

GERTRUDE   ARCHIE   SOPHIE
(PHILIP HOGG)

MR. HORACE DINSMORE SR.
2 nd. WIFE

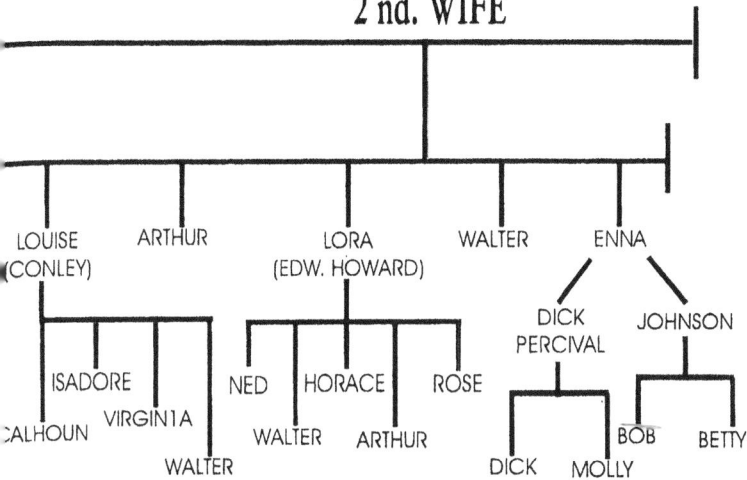

LOUISE (CONLEY)
    ISADORE
    CALHOUN
    VIRGINIA
    WALTER

ARTHUR

LORA (EDW. HOWARD)
    NED
    WALTER
    HORACE
    ARTHUR
    ROSE

WALTER

ENNA
    DICK PERCIVAL
      DICK
      MOLLY
    JOHNSON
      BOB
      BETTY

THE FAMILY
MR. & MRS. ALLISON

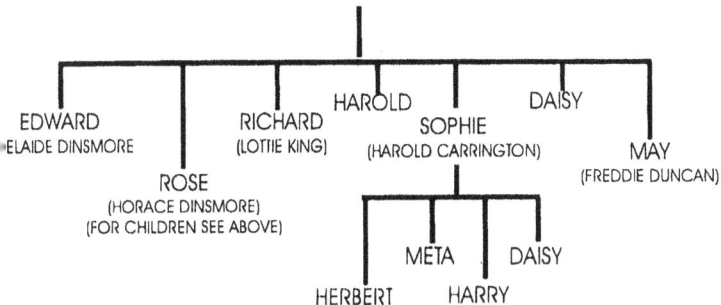

EDWARD (ADELAIDE DINSMORE)

ROSE (HORACE DINSMORE) (FOR CHILDREN SEE ABOVE)

RICHARD (LOTTIE KING)

HAROLD

SOPHIE (HAROLD CARRINGTON)
    HERBERT
    META
    HARRY
    DAISY

DAISY

MAY (FREDDIE DUNCAN)

Elsie's Journey on Inland Waters

A SEQUEL TO
ELSIE AT THE WORLD'S FAIR
BOOK 20

BY
Martha Finley

Complete Authorized Edition

Sovereign Grace Publishers, Inc.
P.O. Box 4998
Lafayette, IN 47903
Phone: (765) 429-4122
Fax: (765) 429-4142

ELSIE'S JOURNEY ON INLAND WATERS.

CHAPTER I.

AFTER her return from the trip across the lake with the bridal party, the *Dolphin* lay at anchor near the White City for a week or more; there were so many interesting and beautiful exhibits at the Fair still unseen by them that Captain Raymond, his family, and guests scarce knew how to tear themselves away.

At the breakfast table on the morning after their arrival, they, as usual, considered together the question where the day should be spent. It was soon evident that they were not all of one mind, some preferring a visit to one building, some to another.

"I should like nothing better than to spend some hours in the Art Palace, examining paintings and statuary," said Violet, "and I have an idea that mamma would enjoy doing the same," looking enquiringly at her mother as she finished her sentence.

"In which you are quite right," responded Grandma Elsie. "There is nothing I enjoy more than pictures and statuary such as may be found there."

"And I am sure your father and I can echo that sentiment," remarked Mrs. Dinsmore, with a smiling glance at her husband.

"Very true, my dear," he said.

"Then that is where we shall go," said the captain.

"That includes your four children, I suppose, papa?" remarked Lucilla, half enquiringly, half in assertion.

"Unless one or more of them should prefer to remain at home—here on the yacht," he replied. "How about that, Neddie, my boy?"

"Oh, papa, I don't want to stay here! Please let me go with you and mamma," exclaimed the little fellow, with a look of mingled alarm and entreaty.

"You certainly shall, if you want to, my son," returned his father. "I am happy to say that my little boy has been very good and given no unnecessary trouble in visiting the Fair thus far. And I can say the same of my little Elsie and her older sisters also," he added, with an affectionate look from one to another.

"Thank you, papa," said Lucilla and Grace, the latter adding, "I think it would be strange indeed should we ever intentionally and willingly give trouble to such a father as ours."

"I don't intend ever to do that," said little Elsie earnestly, and with a loving upward look into her father's face.

"I am glad to hear it, dear child," he returned, with an appreciative smile.

"I, too," said her mother. "Well, we will make quite a party, even if all the rest choose to go elsewhere."

The Art Palace was a very beautiful building of brick and steel; its style of architecture Ionic of the most classic and refined type. It was very large: 320 feet wide by 500 feet in length, with an eastern and western annex, a grand nave and transept 160 feet wide and 70 feet high intersecting it, and that surmounted by a dome very high and wide, and having upon its apex a winged figure of Victory.

From this dome the central section was flooded with light, and here was a grand collection of sculpture and paintings, in which every civilized nation was represented, the number of pieces shown being nearly twenty-five thousand. It was the largest art exhibition ever made in the history of the world.

It was not strange, therefore, that though our

friends had been in the building more than once before, they still found an abundance of fine works of art which were well worth attentive study, and as entirely new to them as though they had been but just placed there.

Little Elsie was particularly attracted, and her curiosity was excited by an oil painting among the French exhibits of Joan of Arc listening to the voices.

"Is there a story to it?" she asked of her grandma, who stood nearest to her at the moment.

"Yes, dear; and if you want to hear it, I shall tell it to you when we go back to the *Dolphin*," was the kindly rejoinder, and the child, knowing that Grandma Elsie's promises were sure to be kept, said no more at the moment, but waited patiently until the appointed time.

As usual, she and Neddie were ready for a rest sooner than the older people, and were taken back to the yacht by their father, Grandma Elsie and Grace accompanying them, saying that they, too, were weary enough to enjoy sitting down with the little folks for an hour or so.

"Oh, I'm glad grandma's going too!" cried Ned, and Elsie added, with a joyous look, "So am I, grandma, but I'm very sorry you are tired."

"Do not let that trouble you, dearest," returned Mrs. Travilla, with a loving smile. "You know if I were not tired I should miss the enjoyment of resting."

"And there is enjoyment in that," remarked the captain; "yet I regret, mother, that your strength is not sufficient to enable you to see and enjoy all the beautiful sights here, which we may never again have an opportunity to behold."

"Well, captain, one cannot have everything in this world," returned Grandma Elsie, with a contented little laugh, "and it is a real enjoyment to me to sit on the deck of the *Dolphin* with my dear little grandchildren about me, and entertain them with such stories as will both interest and instruct them."

"Oh, are you going to tell us the story of that picture I asked you about, grandma?" queried little Elsie, with a look of delight.

"What picture was that?" asked her father, who had not heard what passed between the lady and the child while gazing together upon Maillart's painting.

Mrs. Travilla explained, adding, "I suppose you have no objection to my redeeming my promise?"

"Oh, no! not at all; it is a historical story, and I do not see that it can do them any harm to hear it, sadly as it ends."

They had reached the yacht while talking, and presently were on board and comfortably seated underneath the awning on the deck. Then the captain left them, and Grandma Elsie, noting the look of eager expectancy on little Elsie's face, at once began the coveted tale.

"The story I am about to tell you," she said, "is of things done and suffered more than four hundred years ago. At that time there was war between the English and French. The King of England, not satisfied with his own dominions, wanted France also and claimed it because his mother was the daughter of a former French king; so he sent an army across the Channel into France to force the French to take him for their king, instead of their own monarch."

"Didn't the French people want to have the English king to be theirs too, grandma?" asked Elsie.

"No, indeed! and so a long, long war followed, and a great many of both the French and English were killed.

"At that time there was a young peasant girl named Joan, a modest, industrious, pious girl, who loved her country and was distressed over the dreadful war going on in it. She longed to help to drive the English away; but it did not seem as if she—a girl of fifteen, who could neither read nor write, though she could sew and spin and work out in the fields and gardens—could do anything to help to rid her dear land of the invaders. But she thought a great deal about it and at length imagined that she heard heavenly voices calling to her to go and fight for her king."

"And that was the picture that we saw to-day, grandma?" asked Elsie. "But it wasn't really true?"

"No, dear; probably Joan of Arc, as she is called, really imagined she heard them, and the painter has imagined how they might have looked."

"Then it isn't real," remarked the little girl, in a tone of disappointment.

"No, not what the picture represents; but the story of what poor Joan of Arc, or the Maid of Orleans, as she is often called, thought and did is true. When she told her story of the voices speaking to her no one believed it; they thought she was crazy. But she was not discouraged. She went to her king, or rather the dauphin, for he had not been crowned, and told her story to him and his council—that God had revealed to her that the French troops would succeed in driving the enemy away from the city of Orleans, which they were besieging at that time.

"The dauphin listened, believed what she told him, and gave her leave to dress herself in male attire and go with the troops, riding on a white palfrey and bearing a sword and a white banner. The soldiers believed in her, and in consequence were filled with such courage and enthusiasm that they fought very bravely and soon succeeded in driving the English away from Orleans.

"This success so delighted the French, and so raised their hope of ridding France of her enemies, that they won victory after victory, driving the English out of one province after another, and even out of Paris itself, so that the English hated and dreaded poor Joan.

"She conducted the dauphin to Rheims, where he was crowned, and she wept for joy as she saluted him as king. Then she wanted to go home, thinking her work was done; but King Charles begged her to stay with the army, and to please him she did. But she began to have fearful forebodings because she no longer heard the voices. Yet she remained with the French army and was present at a good many battles, till at length she was taken prisoner by the Burgundians and sold to the English for a large sum by the Burgundian officer."

"Oh, grandma! and did the English hurt her for fighting for her own dear country?"

"I cannot say certainly," replied Mrs. Travilla; "accounts differ, some saying that she was put to death as a heretic and sorceress; others that some five or six years later she arrived at Metz, was at once recognized by her two brothers, and afterward married."

"Oh, I hope that is the true end of the story!" exclaimed Elsie. "It would be so dreadful to have her put to death for helping to save her dear country."

"So it would," said Grace; "but in those early times such dreadful, dreadful deeds used to be done. I often feel thankful that I did not live in those days."

"Yes," said Mrs. Travilla, "we may well be full of gratitude and love to God our Heavenly Father that our lot has been cast in these better times and in our dear land."

"And that we have our dear, kind grandma to love," said Neddie, nestling closer to her, "and our papa and mamma. Some little children haven't any."

"No, I had no mother when I was your age, Ned," sighed Grandma Elsie, "and I cannot tell you how much I used to long for her when Aunt Chloe would tell me how sweet and lovely she had been, and how sorry she was to leave her baby."

"Her baby? was that you, grandma?" he

asked, with a wondering look up into her face.

"Yes," she replied, with a smile, and stroking his hair caressingly.

"But you had a papa? grandpa is your papa, isn't he? I hear you call him that sometimes."

"Yes, he is; my dear father and your mamma's grandfather, which makes him yours too."

"Mine, too," said little Elsie, in a tone of satisfaction.

"Oh, see! here comes the boat with Evelyn and Uncle Walter in it!"

"You are early to-night as well as ourselves," remarked Grace, as they stepped upon the deck and drew near the little group already gathered there.

"Yes," returned Evelyn, "I was tired, and Walter kindly brought me home. The yacht seems like a home to me nowadays," she added, with a light laugh.

"Yes," said Grace; "I am sure papa likes to have us all feel that it is a home to us at present."

"And a very good and comfortable one it is," remarked Walter, handing Evelyn to a seat, then taking one himself opposite her and near his mother's side.

"Where have you two been? and what have you seen that is worth telling about?" asked Grace.

"Visiting buildings," returned Walter; "Brazil, Turkey, Hayti, Sweden, and lastly Venezuela."

"And what did you see there?"

"In Venezuela's exhibit? Christopher Columbus and General Bolivar—that is, their effigies—specimens of birds, animals, minerals, preserves, spices, coffee, vegetables, fine needlework, some manufactured goods, and —most interesting of all, we thought—the flag carried by Pizarro in his conquest of Peru."

"Pizarro? who was he? and what did he do, Uncle Wal?" asked little Elsie.

"He was a very, very bad man and did some very, very wicked deeds," replied Walter.

"Did he kill people?"

"Yes, that he did; and got killed himself at last. The Bible says, 'Whoso sheddeth man's blood, by man shall his blood be shed,' and there have been a great many examples of it in the history of the world."

"Does God say that, Uncle Walter?" asked Neddie.

"Yes; God said it to Noah, shortly after he and his family came out of the ark."

"When the flood was over?"

"Yes."

"Please tell us about that flag and the bad man that carried it," urged little Elsie, and Walter complied.

"Pizarro was a Spaniard," he began, "a very courageous, but covetous and cruel man; very ignorant, too; he could neither read nor write. He was a swineherd in his youth, but gave up that occupation and came over to America to seek a fortune in this new world. He crossed the Isthmus of Panama with Balboa and discovered the Pacific Ocean. While there he heard rumors of a country farther south, where gold and silver were said to be as abundant as iron in Spain, and he was seized with a great desire to go there and help himself to as much as possible. So he and another fellow named Almagro, and Luque, a priest, put their money together and fitted out a small expedition, of which Pizarro took command.

"They did not go very far that time, but afterward tried it again, first making an agreement that all they got of lands, treasures, and other things, vassals included, should be divided equally between them.

"They set sail in two ships. They really reached Peru, and when Pizarro went back to Panama he carried with him many beautiful and valuable ornaments of gold and silver which the kind-hearted natives had given him, also specimens of cloth made of wool and having a silky appearance and brilliant color, and some llamas, or alpacas."

"They had certainly treated him very kindly," remarked Grace, as Walter paused for a moment in his narrative.

"Yes; and what a mean wretch he must have been to want to rob them of everything—even to life, liberty, and happiness. He was determined to do that as soon as possible; so determined that, not being able to find enough volunteers in Panama, he went all the way back to Spain (a far greater undertaking then than it would be now), told the story of his discoveries before the king, Charles V., and his ministers; describing the wealth of the countries and showing the goods and ornaments he had brought from them.

"Then they gave him—what was not theirs to give—permission to conquer Peru, and the titles of governor and captain-general of that country. He on his part agreed to raise a certain number of troops, and to send to the King of Spain one-fifth of all the treasures he should obtain. He then returned to Panama and soon set sail for Peru again."

"With a great many soldiers, Uncle Wal?" queried little Ned.

"No; with what in these days would be considered a very small army; only 180 soldiers, of whom 27 were cavalry."

"Cavalry?" repeated Ned, in a tone of enquiry.

"Yes, soldiers on horseback. The Peruvians, having never before seen a horse, took each mounted man and the steed he rode to be but one animal, and were much afraid of them. The firearms, too, inspired great terror, as they knew nothing of gunpowder and its uses.

"At that time there was war among the natives of Peru and Quito. Huano Capac, the former Inca of Peru, had died some years previous, leaving Peru to his son Huascar, and Quito, which he had conquered shortly before, to another son—half-brother to Huascar. The two had quarrelled and had been fighting each other for about two years, and just before the arrival of the Spaniards Atahualpa had defeated his brother Huascar, taken him prisoner, and confined him in a strong fortress."

"Perhaps," remarked Evelyn, "if they had not been so busy fighting each other they might have discovered the approach of Pizarro, their common enemy, in season to prevent the mischief he was prepared to do them."

"Very possibly," returned Walter. "As it was, the Spaniards drew near Atahualpa's victorious camp, where they found fifty thousand

men assembled. Pizarro had at the most only
two hundred; a mere handful in comparison with
the numbers of the Peruvians, but by a most
daring and diabolical stratagem he got possession of the unsuspecting Inca.

"Atahualpa came to visit him in a friendly
spirit. A priest began explaining to him the
Christian, or rather the papal religion; told
him that the Pope had power over all the king-
doms of the earth and that he had presented
Peru to the King of Spain; also that they had
come to take possession in the name of that
king.

"Naturally that made Atahualpa very angry;
so angry that he indignantly interrupted the
priest, saying that the Pope—whoever he was—
must be a crazy fool to talk of giving away
countries which did not belong to him. Then
he asked on what authority such claims were
made.

"The priest pointed to a Bible. Atahualpa
dashed it angrily to the ground, and the fields
began to fill with Indians. Then Pizarro
waved a white scarf—the signal he had agreed
upon with his men—and his artillery poured
sudden death into the terrified masses of
Indians, while the Spanish cavalry rode them
down in a furious, merciless way. The ranks
of the poor, unarmed Peruvians were thrown

into confusion; their foes were butchering them without mercy; they could do little to save themselves; they used every effort to defend and save the sacred Inca, but in vain; and after hours of that fiendish murdering of the poor, defenceless creatures, the Spaniards got full possession of him.

"At first they pretended to be very kind to him, especially when he offered, as his ransom, to fill the room in which he stood with gold as high as he could reach.

"Huascar, in his prison, heard of this and offered a still larger ransom for himself, and to prevent it Atahualpa had him secretly murdered.

"Soon after that the gold for Atahualpa's ransom began to pour in, and when there was as much as he had promised he demanded his freedom. But Pizarro refused to let him go—though he took the gold—accusing him of plotting against him; and after much base treachery the Spaniards held a mock trial and condemned Atahualpa to be burned. But when they led him out to the stake he consented to be baptized, and for that they were so very merciful as to strangle before burning him."

"Oh, Uncle Walter, what cruel, cruel men!" exclaimed little Elsie.

"They were, indeed," sighed her grandma.

"The Bible tells us 'the tender mercies of the wicked are cruel.' Pizarro and his band were very, very wicked men. They had no more right to the country of the Peruvians than the Peruvians would have had to theirs, had they crossed the ocean to Spain and seized upon it for their own. 'All they that take the sword shall perish with the sword,' our Saviour said, and how true it proved in the case of these men of whom we have been talking! Atahualpa caused his brother Huascar to be killed; Pizarro, Almagro, and the others killed Atahualpa; Pizarro afterward killed Almagro; and later on Pizarro was himself slain by Almagro's son Diego."

CHAPTER II.

NED had begun to nod, and Elsie's eyes drooped as if she too were in need of a nap; perceiving which Grandma Elsie bade their nurse take them to their berth.

A light breeze had sprung up, and it was very pleasant on deck in the shade of the awning; while, resting upon couches or in easy chairs, they talked in a quiet way of the various interesting exhibits to which they had given their attention since leaving the yacht that morning.

"We visited the Illinois Building," said Evelyn, "and were very much interested in the wonderful grain picture there. It is an ideal prairie farm—with farmhouse, barn, stock-sheds, all made of corn-husks as well as the picket fence surrounding it; there are stock and poultry in the barnyard; there is a wind-mill too, and there are fields and cattle."

"Yes," said Walter, as Eva paused in her account, "and the perspective showed fields of grass and grain, pasture too, and sky effects—all made of natural grains, grasses, leaves, and berries indigenous to Illinois."

18

"Oh, I think I must get papa to take us to see it!" exclaimed Grace.

"There is a curtain that partly covers the picture," continued Walter; "it is made of the same materials and caught up by a rope with tassels made of yellow corn.

"We visited the Idaho Building too," he went on, "and I think you should all see it. It is really picturesque—a log-house on a foundation of lava and basaltic rock. The timbers we were told are from young cedar trees, stuffed and stained to produce the effect of age; then it has fine upper and lower balconies shaded by a projecting roof upheld by brackets of logs. I heard people remarking that it was the handsomest log-house ever built, and certainly I never saw any other nearly so handsome."

"Ah, here comes the boat again with the rest of our folks!" exclaimed Grace, and springing to his feet, Walter hastened to the side of the vessel to assist the ladies in getting on board.

"Well, Lu, have you had a good time since I left you?" asked Grace, in a lively tone, as her sister drew near.

"Yes; yes, indeed!" returned Lucilla; "we have seen and enjoyed a great deal, and I wouldn't have missed it on any account, though we are all very tired, I think. I am, I know," she concluded, dropping into a seat by Grace's side.

"As we all are," said Violet. "I am glad, mamma, that you came back to the yacht when you did."

"Yes, I thought it wiser not to allow myself to become very weary before taking rest; and we have had a pleasant, quiet time here together," returned Grandma Elsie, looking up with an affectionate smile into the face of her father, who had just drawn near and was standing by her side, regarding her with a slightly anxious look.

"I am glad you were so prudent," he said, "for you have not been over strong since that illness that made us all so anxious."

"No; and we all feel that we must be very careful of our dear mother," remarked the captain, who had just joined the little group.

"Of Gracie also," he added, smiling down into her face and laying a caressing hand for a moment on her head. "Are you feeling very tired, daughter?"

"Not so very much now, papa," she answered brightly; "we have been resting nicely here, talking over the sights and historical stories connected with them."

Then, turning to her sister, "Tell us where

you have been and what you have seen since we left the party, Lu," she requested.

"Ah, I am afraid I cannot begin to tell all," returned Lucilla, in a lively tone and with a pleased little laugh, "for 'their name is legion'; the loveliest pictures and statuary in the Fine Arts Building, and a great variety of curious and interesting things in Machinery Hall. We went up to the gallery there and took a ride in the travelling crane. It is like an elevated railroad, is moved by electricity, and runs the whole length of the building, twenty or thirty feet above the floor. We stepped in at one end and sat down upon chairs ranged along the front edge, and it was really entertaining to watch the crowds of people moving along the floors below, and to get at last a glance at the exhibits."

"Exhibits!" echoed Grace. "Of what kind? Oh, machines, of course! But I should hardly expect them to be very interesting."

"Machines for making ice-cream and candy would interest you, wouldn't they?" asked Lulu. "Perhaps the hot baths, too; though I suppose you wouldn't care much about printing-presses, rock-drills, sewing-machines, washing-machines, looms, and the like. I own I didn't care over much for them myself. But in the restful, cooling, breezy ride, with nothing to do but watch the goings on of other people, and a glance now and then at something interesting as we glided past it, I did find a good deal of enjoyment. Ah," drawing out her pretty little watch and glancing at its face, "I must excuse myself now and go to my stateroom; for I see it is nearly meal time, and my hair and dress certainly need some attention;" and with that she left them.

Mr. Dinsmore and the captain, wishing to look at some exhibits in which the ladies took but little interest, went ashore again early in the evening; leaving Mrs. Dinsmore, Mrs. Travilla, and the younger ones occupying the comfortable seats on the *Dolphin's* deck, and enjoying the cool evening breeze and the somewhat distant view of the beauties of the brilliantly illuminated White City, as well as that of the starry heavens above them.

Violet had gone down to the cabin with her children to see them safely in bed, and for some minutes no one left in the little group behind had spoken. But presently Grace broke the silence.

"I have just been thinking what a wonderful change has come over this part of our country since the war of 1812. I remember that history tells us there was only a fort and a trading post here then, where now this great city stands, and that it was destroyed. Grandma Elsie, don't you want to tell us the whole story?" she concluded in a coaxing tone.

"I am willing, if you all wish it," was the sweet-toned reply, immediately followed by an eager assent from everyone present.

"Well, then, my dears," she said, "to begin at the beginning—this spot, we are told, was first visited by a white man in 1674. He was a French Jesuit called Father Marquette. He built a cabin there and planted a missionary station. Eleven years afterward his cabin was replaced by a fort. I do not know how long that fort stood, but Lossing tells us that in 1796 a mulatto from St. Domingo found his way to that far-off wilderness, and that the Indians said of him 'the first white man who settled here was a negro.' He did not stay very long, however, and the improvements he had made fell into the hands of the next comer, who was a native of Quebec named John Kinzie.

"He was an enterprising trader with the Indians, and for twenty years the only white man in northern Illinois except a few American soldiers. It was in 1804 that he made Chicago his home, and on the Fourth of July of that year a fort our government had been building there was formally dedicated and called Fort Dearborn, in honor of the then Secretary of War. It stood on a slight elevation on the south bank of the Chicago River, about half a mile from its mouth, and directly opposite, on the north bank, stood Mr. Kinzie's dwelling. It was a modest mansion begun by Jean Baptiste, and enlarged by Mr. Kinzie. He had some Lombardy poplars planted in front within an enclosed yard, and at the back a fine garden and growing orchard.

"There he had lived in peace and prosperity, esteemed and confided in by the surrounding Indians, for eight years, when in June of 1812 war was declared by our government with Great Britain. Of course you all know and remember what were the causes of that second struggle with our mother country?"

"Indeed we do, mother," exclaimed Walter. "She interfered with our commerce, capturing every American vessel bound to, or returning from a port where her commerce was not favored; and worse still, was continually seizing our sailors and forcing them into her service; depriving us of our God-given rights and making slaves of freemen. If ever a war was justifiable on one side that one was on ours. Is it not so?"

"I think it is, my son," replied Grandma Elsie, smiling slightly at the lad's heat.

"Was Fort Dearborn strong and well built, mamma?" queried Rosie.

"Yes; it was strongly picketed, had a block-house at each of two angles on the southern side, on the north side a sally-port and covered way that led down to the river for the double purpose of obtaining water during a siege and of having a way of escape should that be desirable at any time—and was strongly picketed.

"The fort was built by Major Whistler, his soldiers dragging all the timber to the spot because they had no oxen. Some material was furnished from Fort Wayne, but so economically was the work done that the fortress did not cost the government fifty dollars.

"But to return to my story—the garrison there at the time of the declaration of war consisted of fifty-four men. The only other residents of the post at that time were the wives of Captain Heald and Lieutenant Helm, the second in command, those of some of the soldiers, a few Canadians with their wives and children, and Mr. Kinzie and his family.

"They were all on the most friendly terms with the principal tribes of Indians in that neighborhood—the Pottawatomies and Winnebagoes, yet they could not win them from their attachment for the British, who yearly made them large presents as bribes to secure their alliance. Portions of their tribes had been engaged in the battle of Tippecanoe, fought the previous autumn, and since that some of the leading chiefs had seemed sullen, and suspicions of intended hostility on their part at times troubled the minds of the officers of the fort.

"One day in the spring of 1812 two Indians of the Calumet band were at the fort, and seeing Mrs. Helm and Mrs. Heald playing at battledore, one of them, named Nan-non-gee, turned to the interpreter with the remark, 'The white chiefs' wives are amusing themselves very much; it will not be long before they will be living in our cornfields.'"

"Oh!" cried Grace, "I should think that ought to have been enough to warn the officers of the fort to make every preparation to repel an assault by the Indians."

"Yes," said Grandma Elsie, "but Heald seems to have been strangely blind and deaf to every kind of warning.

"On the evening of the 7th of April, 1812, Mr. Kinzie sat by his fireside playing his violin, his children dancing to the music, when their mother, who had been attending a sick neighbor, a Mrs. Burns, living half a mile above the fort, came rushing wildly in crying out: 'The Indians! the Indians!' 'What? where?' exclaimed her husband. 'Up at Lee's, killing and scalping!' she gasped in reply, and went on to tell that the alarm had been given by a boy, the son of Mr. Lee, and a discharged soldier who had been working for them. They had shouted the dreadful tidings across the river to the Burns family, as they ran down the farther side, Mr. Lee's place being between two and three miles farther up the stream.

"Not a moment was to be lost. Mr. Kinzie hurried his family into two pirogues moored in front of his house, and hastened with them across the river and into the fort. The alarm had reached there also, and a scow with Ensign Ronan and six men started at once up the river to rescue the Burns family. Also a cannon was fired to give notice of danger to a party of soldiers who were out fishing. Mrs. Burns and her family, including an infant not yet a day old, were taken safely to the fort."

"I hope those soldiers got back safely too," said Grace.

"Yes; they were two miles above Lee's; it was already dark when they returned, and in passing his house they came upon the bodies of murdered and scalped persons, which were the next day recovered and buried near the fort. It was afterward learned that the scalping party were Winnebagoes from Rock River, who had come with the intention of killing every white person outside of the fort, but were frightened away by the sound of the cannon before they had finished their fiendish work; so fled back to their homes.

"In those days an agency house stood upon the esplanade, about twenty rods west from the fort, and in it all the whites not belonging to the garrison now took refuge. It was an old-fashioned log-house, with a passage through the centre, and piazzas in front and rear extending the whole length of the building. These were planked up, port-holes cut in the barricades and sentinels were posted there every night.

"Hostile Indians hovered around the post for some time, helping themselves to whatever they could lay their hands upon, but at length disappeared, and for a while there was no further alarm.

"On the 7th of August, toward evening, a friendly Pottawatomie chief, named Win-ne-meg, or the Catfish, came to Chicago from Fort Wayne as the bearer of a despatch from General Hull to Captain Heald. In that despatch Hull told of the declaration of war with England, the invasion of Canada, and the loss of Mackinack. It also ordered Captain Heald to evacuate Fort Dearborn, if practicable; and if

he did so to distribute all the United States
property there among the Indians in the neighborhood."

"Including guns, powder, and balls with
which to kill the whites!" said Lucilla. "I
think I should have concluded from such an
order that Hull must be either a traitor or an
idiot."

"His idea," said Grandma Elsie, "seems to
have been to make a peace-offering to the
savages to induce them to refrain from joining
the British, then menacing Detroit.

"Win-ne-meg, who had some knowledge of
the contents of the missive he brought, begged
Mr. Kinzie, with whom he was intimate, to
advise Captain Heald not to evacuate the fort,
assuring him it would prove a difficult and
dangerous movement; for the Indians had
already received information from Tecumseh
of the disasters to the American arms and the
withdrawal of Hull's army from Canada, and
were growing insolent and restless. The fort
was well supplied with ammunition and provisions sufficient to last for six months; by the
end of that time relief might be sent, and why
not hold out till then? But if Heald was resolved to evacuate, it had better be done at once,
before the Indians should be informed of the
order, and so be prepared to make an attack.

"Win-ne-meg's advice in that case was to leave the stores as they were, allowing them to make distribution for themselves; for while they were engaged in that business the white people might make their way in safety to Fort Wayne.

"Mr. Kinzie perceived that this was wise advice, as did the officers of the fort, with the exception of Heald, who would not listen to it, but expressed himself as resolved to yield strict obedience to Hull's orders as to evacuation and the distribution of the public property.

"The next morning Hull's order was read to the troops, and Heald took the whole responsibility of carrying it out. His officers expected to be summoned to a council, but they were not. Toward evening they called upon the commander and remonstrated with him. They said that the march must necessarily be slow on account of the women, children, and infirm persons, therefore, under the circumstances, exceedingly perilous. They reminded him that Hull's order left it to his discretion to go or to stay; adding that they thought it much wiser to strengthen the fort, defy the savages, and endure a siege until help could reach them.

"But Heald replied that he should expect the censure of the government if he remained, for special orders had been issued by the War

Department that no post should be surrendered
without battle having been given by the
assailed; and his force was entirely too small to
hazard an engagement with the Indians. He
added that he had full confidence in the profes-
sions of friendship of many chiefs about him,
and he would call them together, make the
required distribution, then take up his march
for Fort Wayne."

"And did the other officers submit to him
then, Grandma Elsie?" asked Grace.

"Yes; my dear, he was in authority, and I
presume they were too loyal to oppose him.
But being determined to abandon the fort, he
should have done so at once; for delay was certainly increasing the danger, the Indians becoming more unruly every hour; yet he pro-
crastinated and did not call them together for
the final arrangements for two or three days.

"At last that was done and they met near
the fort on the afternoon of the 12th, when
Heald held a farewell council with them. He
invited his officers to join him in that, but they
refused. In some way they had been informed
that treachery was intended on the part of the
Indians, that they had planned to murder them
and then destroy those who were in the fort.
Therefore they remained inside the pickets and
opened a port-hole of one of the block-houses so

that the Indians could see a cannon pointing
directly toward their group, thus protecting
Captain Heald. It had the desired effect; no
effort was made by the savages to carry out
their treacherous design, they professed friendship, and accepted Heald's offers to distribute
among them the goods in the public store—
blankets, calicoes, broadcloths, paints, and
other things such as Indians fancy."

"Beads among them, I presume," remarked
Rosie.

"Very likely," said her mother, "as they
have always been a favorite ornament with the
Indians. The distribution of those goods, the
arms and ammunition and such of the provisions
as would not be needed by the garrison, was to
take place next day; then the whites were to
leave the fort and set out upon their journey
through the wilderness, the Pottawatomies
engaging to furnish them with an escort, on
condition of being liberally rewarded on their
arrival at Fort Wayne."

"Oh, but I should have been afraid to trust
them!" exclaimed Grace, shuddering at the
very thought of the risk.

"Mr. Kinzie, who knew the Indians so well,
was of your opinion," said Grandma Elsie,
"and earnestly remonstrated with Captain
Heald; telling him they were not to be trusted

in the face of such temptations. Especially he urged him not to put arms and ammunition in their hands, as that would fearfully increase their ability to carry on the murderous raids which had become so frequent and caused so great terror in the frontier settlements.

"He succeeded in convincing Heald that he had been very foolish in making that promise, and he resolved to violate his treaty so far as the arms and ammunition were concerned. That very evening something occurred that certainly ought to have opened Heald's eyes and led him to shut the gates of the fort and defend it to the last extremity. Black Partridge, a chief who had thus far always been friendly to the whites, and who was a man of great influence too, came to Heald in a quiet way and said, 'Father, I come to deliver to you the medal I wear. It was given me by the Americans, and I have long worn it in token of our mutual friendship. But our young men are resolved to imbrue their hands in the blood of the white people. I cannot restrain them, and I will not wear a token of peace while I am compelled to act as an enemy.'"

"And did Heald actually disregard such a warning as that?" exclaimed Evelyn Leland. "I really do not see how it could have been made plainer that the purpose was to attack and murder all in the fort as soon as they were fairly in their power."

"Nor do I," said Grandma Elsie; "yet Heald seems to have paid no more attention to it than to the previous warnings.

"The next morning, August 13, was bright and cool. The Indians came in great numbers to receive their promised presents. Only the goods in the store were distributed that day, and in the evening Black Partridge said to Mr. Griffith, the interpreter, ' Linden birds have been singing in my ears to-day; be careful on the march you are going to take.' This was repeated to Captain Heald, but solemn warning as it evidently was, he paid no more attention to it than he had to previous ones. He seems to have been perfectly infatuated, and how he could ever forgive himself in after years I cannot see. He went steadily on in the execution of his plans, of which, as I have told you, all the other officers, Mr. Kinzie, and friendly Indian chiefs disapproved. That night he had all the guns but such as his party could make use of in their journey—gunscrews, flint, shot, and everything belonging to the use of firearms—thrown into the well. This was done at midnight, when the sentinels were posted and the Indians in their camp; at least, they were supposed to be, but the night was dark,

Indians can move noiselessly, and some whose suspicions had been aroused crept to the spot and made themselves acquainted with what was going on. Liquor and powder, too, were poured into the well, and a good deal of alcohol, belonging to Mr. Kinzie, into the river; also a portion of the powder and liquor of the fort was thrown into a canal that came up from the river far under the covered way. But the water of the river was sluggish, and so great a quantity of liquor had been thrown into it that in the morning it was like strong grog; and powder could be seen floating on the surface."

"And of course the Indians, who loved liquor, were angry when they saw how it had been wasted, instead of given to them," remarked Grace.

"Yes; their complaints and threats were loud, and now the little garrison had no choice but to brave the danger of exposing themselves to their vengeance, for it was no longer possible to hold the fort, and they must set out upon their perilous journey. Ah! if Heald had but been less obstinately bent upon having his own way—more willing to listen to the advice and remonstrances of his officers, Kinzie, who understood the Indians so well, and the warning of the friendly chiefs, much suffering might have been averted and valuable lives saved.

"Mrs. Heald had an uncle, the brave Captain William Wells, who had passed most of his life among the Miami Indians and been made one of their chiefs. He had heard at Fort Wayne of Hull's order to evacuate Fort Dearborn, and knowing of the hostility of the Pottawatomies, had made a rapid march across the country with a party of his Miamis to reinforce Heald and help him to hold and defend the fort. But he arrived just too late; the means of defence had already been destroyed, and there was no choice but to attempt the perilous march through the wilderness.

"Nine o'clock of the 15th was the hour set for the evacuation, and it was already evident that the Indians intended to massacre the whites—men, women, and children. Nor could they entertain any hope of being able to defend themselves, so overwhelming was the number of their savage foes, 500 warriors against 54 soldiers, 12 civilians, and 3 or 4 women."

"But there were the Miamis with Wells, mamma," remarked Rosie.

"Who proved of no assistance," returned Grandma Elsie. "Lossing tells us that when, at nine o'clock, the gates were thrown open, and the march began, it was like a funeral procession. The band struck up the Dead March in 'Saul.' Captain Wells, with his friendly Miamis, took

the lead, his face blackened with gunpowder in
token of his impending fate. His niece, Mrs.
Heald, with her husband, came next, while the
others, I presume, followed in the order of
their rank."

"Were the Kinzies with them?" asked
Grace.

"Mr. Kinzie was, hoping by his personal
influence to be able to soften, if not avert their
impending fate. His family had left in a boat,
in charge of a friendly Indian who was to take
them to his other trading station, where Niles,
Mich., now stands. Poor Mrs. Kinzie! having
a daughter among the seemingly doomed ones,
how terribly anxious and distressed she must
have been!" added Grandma Elsie in tones
tremulous with feeling. A moment of silence
followed, then she went on with her narrative.

CHAPTER III.

"THE procession, escorted by the five hundred Pottawatomies, moved slowly along the lake shore in a southerly direction till they had reached the Sand Hills between the prairie and the beach. There the Indians filed to the right, so that the hills were between them and the white people.

"Wells and his mounted Miamis, who were in the advance, came suddenly dashing back, their leader shouting, 'They are about to attack us: form instantly!'

"The words had scarcely left his lips when a storm of bullets came from the Sand Hills. The Pottawatomies, both treacherous and cowardly, had made of those hills a covert from which to attack the little band of whites.

"The troops were hastily brought into line, charged up the hill, and one of their number, a white-haired man of seventy, fell dead from his horse, the first victim of the perfidy of the Indians hounded on by the inhuman Proctor, a worse savage than they.

"The Miamis proved cowardly and fled at the

first onset. Their chief rode up to the **Potta-watomies**, charged them with perfidy, and brandishing his tomahawk told them he would be the first to lead Americans to punish them; then, wheeling his horse, he dashed away over the prairie, following his fleeing companions.

"Both men and women among the whites fought bravely for their lives; they could not hope to save them, but they would sell them to the savage foe as dearly as possible. It was a short, desperate, bloody conflict. Lossing tells us that Captain Wells displayed the greatest coolness and gallantry. At the beginning of the fight he was close beside his niece, Mrs. Heald.

"'We have not the slightest chance for life,' he said to her. 'We must part to meet no more in this world; God bless you!' and with that he dashed forward into the midst of the fight. Seeing a young warrior, painted like a demon, climb into a wagon in which were twelve children, and scalp them all, he forgot his own danger, and burning to avenge the dreadful deed, cried out, 'If butchering women and children is their game, I'll kill too!' at the same time dashing toward the Indian camp where they had left their squaws and papooses.

"Instantly swift-footed young warriors were in hot pursuit, firing upon him as they ran, while he, lying close to his horse's neck, occasionally turned and fired upon them. He had got almost beyond the range of their rifles when a shot killed his horse and wounded him severely in the leg.

"Yelling like fiends the young savages rushed forward to make him prisoner, intending, as he well knew, not to kill him at once, but to reserve him for a lingering and painful death by slow torture. Two Indian friends of his—Win-ne-meg and Wau-ban-see—tried to save him, but in vain; and he, knowing well for what fate he would be reserved if taken alive, taunted his pursuers with the most insulting epithets, to provoke them to kill him instantly.

"He succeeded at last by calling one of them, Per-so-tum by name, a squaw, which so enraged him that he despatched Wells at once with a tomahawk, jumped upon his body, tore out his heart, and ate a portion of it with savage delight."

"Oh, how awful!" cried Grace, shuddering with horror. "How his niece must have felt when she saw it!"

"Very possibly she did not see it," said Grandma Elsie, "so busy as she must have been in defending herself. She was an expert with the rifle and as an equestrienne, defended herself bravely, and received severe wounds; but, though faint and bleeding, managed to keep the saddle. An Indian raised his tomahawk over her and she looked him full in the face, saying, with a melancholy smile, 'Surely you would not kill a squaw!' At that his arm fell, but he took the horse by the bridle and led it toward the camp with her still in the saddle. It was a fine animal, and the Indians had been firing at her in order to get possession of it, till she had received seven bullets in her person. Her captor had spared her for the moment, but as he drew near the camp, his covetousness so overcame his better impulses that he took her bonnet from her head and was about to scalp her when Mrs. Kinzie, sitting in her boat, whence she had heard the sounds of the conflict but could not see the combatants, caught sight of them and cried out to one of her husband's clerks who was standing on the beach, 'Run, run, Chandonnai! That is Mrs. Heald. He is going to kill her. Take that mule and offer it as a ransom.'

"Chandonnai made haste to obey the order, offered the mule and two bottles of whisky in addition, and as the three amounted to more value than Proctor's offered bounty for a scalp, he succeeded, and Mrs. Heald was placed in the boat and there hidden from the eyes of other scalp-hunters."

"I think you were right, Grandma Elsie, in calling that Proctor a worse savage than those Indians! bribing them as he did to murder men, women, and children!" exclaimed Lucilla, her eyes flashing with indignation.

"Is it quite certain that he did?" asked Grace.

"Quite," replied Grandma Elsie. "Lossing tells us that Proctor had offered a liberal sum for scalps, and that in consequence nearly all the wounded men were killed, their scalps carried to him at Malden, and such a bounty paid for them as is given for the destruction of so many wolves. In a footnote Lossing gives an extract from Niles' *Weekly Register* of April 3, 1813, in which it is stated that Mrs. Helm had arrived in Buffalo, and in the narrative she gave of her sufferings at and after the massacre at Chicago said, 'Colonel Proctor, the British commander at Malden, bought the scalps of our murdered garrison at Chicago,' and thanks to her noble spirit, she boldly charged him with the infamy in his own house."

"Did he deny it?" asked Evelyn.

"We are not told that he did; but no doubt he was angered, for he afterward treated both her and her husband with great cruelty, causing them to be arrested and sent across the wilderness from Detroit to Niagara frontier, in the

dead of a Canadian winter. The writer also
stated that Mrs. Heald had learned from the
tribe with whom she was a prisoner, and who
were the perpetrators of those murders, that
they intended to remain true, but received
orders from the British to cut off our garrison
whom they were to escort.

"In our wars with England many British
officers have shown themselves extremely cruel,
—not a whit behind the savages in that respect,—but it would be very wrong to judge of
the whole nation by their conduct; for there
were in the mother country many who felt
kindly toward America and the Americans.
And I think," she added, with her own sweet
smile, "that there are many more now."

"It seems Mrs. Helm too escaped with her
life," said Walter; "but she was wounded, I
presume, mother, since you just spoke of her
sufferings both at and after the massacre."

"Yes, a stalwart young Indian attempted to
scalp her; she sprang to one side, and the blow
from his tomahawk fell on her shoulder instead
of her head; at the same instant she seized him
around the neck and attempted to take his
scalping-knife, which hung in a sheath on his
breast. Before the struggle was ended another
Indian seized her, dragged her to the margin of
the lake, plunged her in, and to her astonish-

ment held her there in a way to enable her to breathe; so that she did not drown. Presently she discovered that he was the friendly Black Partridge, and that he was engaged in saving instead of trying to destroy her life.

"The wife of a soldier named Corbord fought desperately, suffering herself to be cut to pieces rather than surrender; believing that, if taken prisoner, she would be reserved for torture. The wife of Sergeant Holt was another brave woman. At the beginning of the engagement her husband was badly wounded in the neck, and taking his sword she fought like an Amazon. She rode a fine, spirited horse, which the Indians coveted, and several of them attacked her with the butts of their guns, trying to dismount her, but she used her sword with such skill that she foiled them; then suddenly wheeling her horse, she dashed over the prairie, a number of them in hot pursuit and shouting, 'The brave woman! the brave woman! don't hurt her!' "

"Did they overtake her?" asked Grace.

"Yes, at length; when a powerful savage seized her by the neck and dragged her backward to the ground while several others engaged her in front."

"Oh, I hope they didn't kill her!" exclaimed Grace.

"No," replied Mrs. Travilla; "she was afterward ransomed. But to go on with my story. Presently the firing ceased; the little band of whites who had escaped death succeeded in breaking through the ranks of the assassins—who gave way in front—and rallied on the flank, and gained a slight eminence on the prairie near a grove called the Oak Woods. The Indians gathered upon the Sand Hills and gave signs of a willingness to parley. Two-thirds of the whites had been killed or wounded; only 28 strong men remained to cope with the fury of nearly 500 savages—they had lost but 15 in the conflict. To prolong the contest would be little better than madness. Captain Heald, accompanied only by a half-breed boy in Mr. Kinzie's service, went forward and met Black-Bird on the open prairie to arrange terms of surrender.

"It was agreed that all the whites who had survived the conflict should become prisoners of war, to be exchanged as soon as practicable. With this understanding captors and captives all started for the Indian camp near the fort. On arriving there another terrible scene ensued. The Indians did not consider the wounded to be included in the terms of surrender, and immediately proceeded to kill and scalp nearly all of them."

"To gain the bounty offered by that—human, or inhuman fiend Proctor!" exclaimed Walter. "I wonder how he viewed that transaction when he came to die."

"I am sure that in the sight of God he was a wholesale murderer," said Rosie; "a murderer not of men only, but of innocent women and children also."

"Yes," said her mother, "there were twelve children killed, besides Captain Wells, Surgeon Van Voorhees, Ensign Ronan, and twenty-six private soldiers.

"Toward evening the family of Mr. Kinzie were permitted to return to their own home, where they found the friendly Black Partridge waiting for them. Mrs. Helm, the daughter of Mrs. Kinzie, you will remember was his prisoner. He placed her in the house of a Frenchman named Ouilmette. But the Kinzies and all the prisoners were in great danger from a freshly arrived band of Pottawatomies from the Wabash, who were thirsting for blood and plunder. They thoroughly searched Mr. Kinzie's house for victims; but some friendly Indians arrived just in time to prevent the carrying out of their bloodthirsty intentions. These were led by a half-breed chief called Billy Caldwell. Black Partridge told him of the evident purpose of the Wabash Indians, who had blackened their faces and were sitting sullenly in Mr. Kinzie's parlor, no doubt intending presently to start out and engage in the savage work they had planned. Billy went in and said in a careless way, as he took off his accoutrements: 'How now, my friends! A good-day to you! I was told there were enemies here, but I am glad to find only friends. Why have you blackened your faces? Is it that you are mourning for your friends lost in battle? Or is it that you are fasting? If so, ask our friend here (indicating Mr. Kinzie) and he will give you to eat. He is the Indians' friend, and never yet refused them what they had need of.'

"Hearing all this the Wabash Indians were ashamed to own what their intention had been, and so the threatened massacre did not take place. The prisoners were divided among the captors and finally reunited or restored to their friends and families."

"But they must have had a great deal to endure before that happy consummation," sighed Evelyn. "Oh, I think we can never be thankful enough that we live in these better times!"

"So do I," said Grace. "How very dreadful it must be to fall into the hands of savages and meet with a death so awful and sudden! I wish I knew that they were all Christians and ready for heaven."

"I can echo that wish," said Grandma Elsie, in tones full of sadness; "but I very much fear that they were not. Some we may hope were, but it is said, on what seems good authority, that Mrs. Helm, in telling of that terrible scene near the Sand Hills, spoke of the terror of Dr. Van Voorhees. He had been wounded badly, and his horse shot under him, when he asked her, 'Do you think they will take our lives?' and then spoke of offering a large ransom for his. She advised him not to think of that, but of inevitable death. 'Oh, I cannot die! I am not fit to die!' he exclaimed. 'If I had only a short time to prepare for it—death is awful!'"

" 'Look at that man! at least he dies like a soldier,' she said, pointing to Ensign Ronan. 'Yes,' gasped the doctor, 'but he has no terror of the future—he is an unbeliever.'

"Just then Mrs. Helm's struggle with the young Indian who attempted to tomahawk her began, and directly afterward she saw the dead body of Van Voorhees."

"Oh, poor, poor fellow!" exclaimed Grace, tears starting to her eyes. "One would think that, in such circumstances as theirs had been for months, every man and woman would have been careful to make sure work for eternity."

"Yes, but Satan is ever tempting men to delay, and perhaps more souls are, in Christian lands, lost through procrastination than from any other cause," sighed Grandma Elsie. " 'Now is the accepted time; now is the day of salvation.' "

There was a moment of silence, broken by Evelyn.

"I remember when I was a very little girl, papa used to talk to me about being a Christian, and that once I answered him, 'I would, papa, if I only knew how,' and he said, 'It is very simple, daughter; just to believe in the Lord Jesus, take him for your Saviour, and give yourself to him—soul and body, time, talents, influence—all that you have or ever shall have, to be his forever, trusting in him with all your heart, sure that he meant all that he said in speaking to Nicodemus—'God so loved the world that he gave his only begotten Son, that whosoever believeth in him should not perish, but have everlasting life.' And that other, 'Him that cometh to me I will in no wise cast out.' Those two texts seem to me to make the way very simple and plain."

"They do indeed," said Grandma Elsie, "and anyone who has the Bible and will study it faithfully, with earnest prayer to God for help to understand and obey its teachings, can hardly fail to find the way."

CHAPTER IV.

THE greater part of the next day was spent by our friends in a farewell visit to the Fair; but the sun had not yet set when again they all gathered upon the *Dolphin's* deck, and she weighed anchor and proceeded on her course up the lake.

"What a wonderful city it is to be so young!" remarked Mr. Dinsmore when they reached Chicago.

"Yes, sir," said Rosie. "Mamma was giving us a little sketch of its early history, last evening; and we found it very interesting; but I can't say that the events here, or anywhere else, for that matter, of the war of 1812–14 have increased my love for the British. Think of them hiring the Indians to kill men, women, and children, paying just the bounty for them that they would for so many wolf-scalps!"

"Yes, it was barbarous indeed; but do not forget that even in the days of the Revolution there were Britons who viewed such doings with horror. In 1777 there was a debate in the

English Parliament concerning the employment of Indians against the American colonists, when a member of the House of Lords spoke in approval of it, saying it was right to use the means given them by God and Nature. 'God and Nature!' repeated the Earl of Chatham in scornful tones. 'Those abominable principles and this most abominable avowal of them demand most decisive indignation. I call upon that right reverend bench (pointing to the bishops), those holy ministers of the Gospel and pious pastors of the Church—I conjure them to join in the holy work, and to vindicate the religion of their God.' That showed that he (Chatham) was strongly opposed to such barbarity, but his appeal to the bishops was vain. Every man of them voted for the employment of the savages in a war against their brethren, who were fighting for their freedom after years of patient endurance of oppression—years of patient but unsuccessful effort to gain it by peaceful means."

"Yes, I have always admired William Pitt!" said Rosie. "But did any of the British people disapprove of the employment of the Indians in the war of 1812, grandpa?"

"I presume a great many did, though I do not just now remember any historical mention of the fact," replied Mr. Dinsmore, "except among those whose business interests were sure or likely to suffer," he added musingly.

"Those Sand Hills from behind which the Pottawatomies fired upon the whites are quite gone now, are they not, papa?" asked Grace.

"Yes," replied Captain Raymond, "the city now covers the entire theatre of the events of that dreadful day. It has been a rapid and wonderful transformation."

"Don't you think, papa, it might have been saved—I mean Fort Dearborn—if Captain Heald had not been so obstinately determined to do as he thought best, regardless of the opinions of his officers and Mr. Kinzie, and the warnings of friendly Indians?" asked Grace.

"I do, indeed," was the emphatic reply. "And that Mackinack, which fell into the hands of the British about a month earlier, might have been saved to our country but for the criminal neglect of the then Secretary of War. Hancks, who was in command, did not know, had not heard of the declaration of war, though he might have been informed of it nearly a week earlier than the news reached the British commander of Fort St. Joseph, who led the attack, and by reason of the ignorance of the garrison and its commander of the true state of affairs came upon them so unexpectedly that they had no opportunity to defend the fortress."

"Oh, tell us the story of it, papa, please!" pleaded little Elsie, and drawing her to a seat upon his knee, he complied at once.

"The fort was built in the first place by the French," he said, "and taken from them by the English when they conquered Canada. The Indians were not pleased with the change and said to the English, 'You have conquered the French, but you have not conquered us.' Perhaps you may remember what I told you some weeks ago about the attack of the Indians upon the people in the fort. The Indians were playing ball outside the walls of the fortress, and, pretending to be very friendly, invited the garrison to view the game. It was a gay and exciting scene, and the unsuspicious members of the garrison were looking on with interest, forgetting to be on their guard against treachery, when a ball went up in a lofty curve and fell near the pickets of the fort.

"It was a preconcerted signal; the warriors instantly rushed toward the fort, armed with hatchets which their squaws had concealed under their blankets, and the whites being taken by surprise, a dreadful massacre followed.

"The following year the fort was again garrisoned by the English, the Indians fleeing at their approach. After the Revolutionary War —in 1796—the island with its fort came into possession of the United States, the western military posts being surrendered to the Americans by the British, and in 1812 the fortress, then called Fort Holmes, was garrisoned by fifty-seven men under the command of Lieutenant Hancks of the United States Artillery. As a defence of the fur-traders and the scattered settlements of the Northwest, it was a very important post. You doubtless remember that it stands on a bluff overlooking the harbor."

"It is a beautiful place in the summer," remarked Grace, "but must be dreary enough through the long winters."

"It is," said her father, "yet by no means so dreary now as it was in those days, surrounded by hordes of savages ever ready to raise the hatchet in the pay of those who seemed to be the stronger party.

"Lieutenant Hancks and his garrison knew that in the event of war they must be prepared to defend themselves, but as you have just been told, they were left in uncertainty for nearly a week after the news should have reached them. There had been rumors of expected hostilities brought by traders, but the first intimation that there had been an actual

declaration of war was given by the arrival of
the English Captain Roberts, on the morning
of the 17th of July, with his garrison of British
regulars—46, including 4 officers—260 Canadian militia, and 715 Indians—Ottawas, Chip-
pewas, Sioux, Winnebagoes.

"They came in boats, bateaux, canoes, con-
voyed by the brig *Caledonia*, which belonged
to the Northwest Fur Company and was laden
with provisions and stores.

"On the morning of the day before, the Indian
interpreter had told Hancks he had reliable information that the Indians were assembling in
large numbers at St. Joseph and were about
to attack Fort Holmes.

"Hancks had no sooner heard that than he
summoned the American gentlemen on the
island to a conference on the matter, at which
it was decided to send a messenger to St.
Joseph to learn, if possible, the temper of the
commandant, and to watch the movements of
the Indians.

"Captain Darman was the man chosen, and
he set off upon his errand about sunset that
same evening."

"All by himself, papa, when it was just getting dark, too?" asked Elsie. "How could he
see to row his boat?"

"A full moon shone in the sky, daughter, and

lighted him on his way," replied the captain. "But he had gone only fifteen miles when he met the boats carrying the British and Indians, and was taken prisoner by them."

"And did they kill him and scalp him, papa?"

"No; they let him go on condition that he would return to the island in advance of them, call the people together to the west side of it to receive the protection of a British guard for themselves and their property, and not give Lieutenant Hancks any information of the approach of the enemy. Also he was to warn the people that if any of them carried the news to the fort there would be a general massacre. Darman was landed at dawn, and did exactly as he had promised."

"Oh, papa! and didn't anybody warn the poor fellows in the fort?"

"Yes; a Dr. Day, braver than any of the rest, hurried to the fort and gave the alarm while the others were fleeing from the village to escape from the bloodthirsty savages. But it was too late; the enemy had already landed and taken one of their two heavy guns to the top of the hill at the back of the fort, placing it so as to command the American works at their weakest point. By nine o'clock Roberts had possession of the heights, and hideously painted savages were swarming everywhere.

"At half-past eleven the Americans were summoned to surrender the fortress to the forces of his 'Britannic Majesty.' Hancks then held a consultation with his officers and the American gentlemen in the fort, and all agreeing in the opinion that it would be impossible to defend it against such overwhelming numbers —over a thousand, while the garrison could boast but fifty-seven men rank and file—he decided that it was expedient to surrender.

"Honorable terms were granted and at noon the American colors were taken down and those of Great Britain substituted in their stead. The prisoners were all paroled, and those who desired to leave the island were sent in a British vessel to Detroit."

"I should hardly have supposed any American would want to stay here under British rule," remarked Grace.

"An order was presently issued that all upon the island who would not take the oath of allegiance to the British government must leave there within a month," said Captain Raymond.

"And they didn't let the Indians kill anybody, papa?" asked Elsie.

"No," replied her father, "but it is altogether likely that if there had been any resistance many, if not all, would have fallen victims to the bloodthirsty savages, for one of the

British, who had command of 280 of the Indians, said in a letter to Colonel Claus at Fort George, 'It was a fortunate circumstance that the fort surrendered without firing a single gun, for had they done so, I firmly believe not a soul would have been saved.'"

"The capture of Mackinaw was a great loss to our country, was it not, father?" asked Lucilla.

"Yes, it was indeed," responded the captain, "a loss to the fur-trade of the West and a terrible calamity to the people of Detroit and other Western pioneers. It gave the enemy command of the upper lakes with all the advantages connected with it, and exposed Detroit to fearful raids by the hostile Indians."

"And all that dreadful state of affairs was the result of the unpardonable negligence of the Secretary of War!" she exclaimed. "Really, I don't see how he could ever forgive himself."

"No, nor do I," said Rosie, "especially when afterward Detroit too fell into the hands of the British; for its fall was a great assistance to the British cause."

"Yes," said Walter, "in more ways than one; for they got arms, ammunition, and stores; also it was months before another invading army of Americans could be raised and furnished with arms and other necessaries; and in the meantime the British made their preparations for further attacks upon us. They got valuable stores at Mackinaw, too; among them seven hundred packages of costly furs. By the way, Brother Levis, was there not an attempt made by our troops, later on in the war, to repossess Mackinaw?"

"Yes; Mackinaw was the key to the traffic in furs of the Northwest; therefore the Americans were determined to recapture it, and the British fully as determined to keep possession of it; for which purpose they sent there a considerable body of troops consisting of regulars, Canadian militia, and seamen. They took with them twenty-four bateaux loaded with ordnance, and found on the island a large body of Indians waiting to join them as allies. That was in April, 1814, and about the same time Commander Arthur St. Clair with a little squadron consisting of the *Caledonia, St. Lawrence, Niagara, Tigress,* and *Scorpion,* started on a land and naval expedition to the upper lakes. The land force, under the command of Lieutenant-colonel Croghan, the gallant defender of Fort Stephenson, was attacked by the British and Indians August 1, 1813."

"Oh, yes, I remember!" exclaimed Walter. "What splendid work he did there, though he was but twenty-one years old!"

"The expedition left Detroit early in July," continued the captain. "I will not go into the whole story of its action at present; sufficient to say they arrived at Mackinaw on the 26th of July. They soon learned that the enemy was very strong in position and numbers, and it was a question between St. Clair and Croghan whether it would be wise to make an immediate attack. The guns of the vessels could not damage the works because they were so elevated, and they could not carry the place by storm.

"Finally it was decided that Croghan should land on the western side of the island, under cover of the guns of the vessels, and try to attack the works in the rear. He did so on the 4th of August, landing without much molestation, but was presently met by the garrison, who were strongly supported by the Indians in the thickets; also a storm of shot and shell was poured upon them from a battery of guns. There was a sharp fight and Croghan was compelled to fall back and return to the ship; 1 officer and 12 privates had been killed, 52 wounded, and 2 others were missing.

"The attempt to recover Mackinaw at that time had to be given up, and most of the little squadron sailed for Detroit. The *Scorpion* and the *Tigress* were left behind to blockade the

only route by which provisions and other supplies could reach Mackinaw. The two vessels
cruised about for some time till the garrison
was threatened with starvation or surrender in
order to avert it; but early in September they
were both captured by British and Indians sent
out from the fort. They came in five boats and
surprised the *Tigress* first, when the *Scorpion*
was said to be fifteen miles away. She was at
anchor near the shore, it was about nine o'clock
in the evening, intensely dark, and the enemy
was within fifty yards of the vessel when discovered.

"The Americans made a gallant defence, but
were overpowered by numbers, there being but
thirty of them beside the officers, and about
one hundred of the assailants. Lieutenant
Bulger, the British commander of the expedition, said in his report of the affair that the
defence of the vessel did credit to her officers,
who were all severely wounded. They and the
crew were all sent prisoners of war to Mackinaw, while Bulger and his men remained on
board the *Tigress.* They kept her position
unchanged and her pennant flying, and when,
on the 5th, the *Scorpion* was seen approaching,
Bulger ordered his men to hide.

"All this deceived the men on the *Scorpion;*
they thought the *Tigress* was still in the hands

of their comrades, and when within two miles anchored for the night. At dawn the next morning the British ran the *Tigress* down alongside of her, the concealed soldiers ran out from their hiding-places, rushed on board the *Scorpion*, and in a few minutes the British flag was floating over her."

"And the British were very jubilant over the capture, as I remember reading," remarked Violet.

"And not very truthful in their report of it," added Walter. "Lossing says Adjutant-General Baynes actually reported in a general order that the vessels had crews of 300 each; only exaggerating 570 in stating the aggregate of the crews of the two schooners."

But just here the talk was interrupted by the not unwelcome summons to their evening meal.

CHAPTER V.

As they left the table and gathered upon deck on the evening of the next day, the captain announced that they were nearing Mackinaw.

"I am glad of that, papa," said Grace; "for we shall have a lovely view of it by moonlight."

"Are we going to stop there, sir?" asked Walter.

"Not unless someone particularly desires it," returned the captain; "but we will pass slowly and quite near, so that we may all have a good view of it. Ah! it can be seen in the distance now," he added, pointing it out.

"And though the sun has set the moon will, as Gracie says, give us a lovely view of it," remarked Violet.

"Yes, she is nearly full," said the captain, glancing skyward, "which will help us to a more vivid conception of how things looked to Darman when he set out for Fort St. Joseph, on the 16th of July, 1812."

"I'm glad of that," said Lucilla. "I want to

be able to imagine just how things looked at that time."

"Yes," said Grace, "but it is far more delightful to know that no war is going on now, and we are in no danger from either civilized or savage foes."

"It is indeed!" responded her father. "Peace is a great blessing; war a dreadful scourge."

"It is an Indian name the island bears, is it not, captain?" asked Evelyn.

"Yes; and the meaning is the Great Turtle, alluding to its shape. Notice that as we approach, and see if you do not think the name appropriate."

"To the tongue of which of the Indian tribes does the name belong, sir?" asked Walter.

"The Algonquin."

"The harbor is considered a fine one, is it not?"

"Yes; it is semicircular, 1 mile long; the strait is 40 miles long and 4 miles wide; the island 7 miles in circumference. Now we are near enough for a good view."

"What makes it look so white, papa?" queried little Elsie.

"It is limestone rock, my child," replied her father. "See the village down near the water and the fort on higher ground—the white cliffs

half covered with green foliage—beyond it the
ruins of old Fort Holmes."

"The one the British took in that war you
told about, papa?"

"The very same," he said. "I believe you
were not by when I pointed it out to the others
on our former visit to the island."

"No, sir; I think Neddie and I were asleep
in our berths."

"Yes, so you were," said her mother. "Ah,
my dear," to her husband, "what a lovely sight
it is by this witching light!"

"Yes," he said. "I think we will visit it
again one of these days, when we can spend
more time in viewing the various interesting
places—such as the Arch Rock, a natural
bridge almost as picturesque as the famous one
in Virginia, the Rabbit's Peak, Giant's Cause-
way, and the Lover's Leap. We are passing
that last now; and I want you all to notice a
projecting crag at the other end of the island,
called Robinson's Folly. These are all famous
places, and each has its legendary story."

They steamed slowly past, greatly enjoying
the moonlight view of the island; then, as it
faded from sight, the speed of the vessel was
increased, and before the older ones had retired
they had entered Lake Huron.

The pleasant weather continued, and most of

them spent the greater part of the following day upon the deck.

"We will reach Detroit early this evening, I suppose, Brother Levis?" said Rosie, in a tone of enquiry.

"Should nothing happen to prevent," was the pleasant-toned reply. "And now I wonder if my pupils can tell us most of the history of that city?"

"Beginning with the war of 1812, I suppose, as we have already gone over the story of the doings of Pontiac?"

"Yes; but first I shall give you a few facts concerning its settlement, growth, and so forth:

"It is by far the oldest city in the western part of our country, and older than either Philadelphia or Baltimore on the seaboard. It was founded by the French in 1670, as an out-post for the prosecution of the fur-trade ; and as late as 1840 it still had less than 10,000 inhabitants. It is on the west side of Detroit River, about 7 miles from Lake St. Clair and 18 from Lake Erie. Can you tell me the meaning of the name Detroit, Elsie, daughter?"

"No, papa, you never taught me that," replied the little girl.

"It is the French for strait," he said. "The strait or river connecting Lakes St. Clair and Erie gave the name to the city."

"At the time we are talking of—when General Hull was marching toward the place—Detroit had only 160 houses and a population of about 800, most of them of French descent. It was a very small place considering its age, for it was a trading-post as early as 1620, and established as a settlement as early as 1701, when a Jesuit missionary came there with one hundred men. So it was a very old town though so small; but seven years before there had been a fire that destroyed all the houses but one."

"But there was a fort, was there not, papa?" asked Grace.

"Yes," replied the captain; "on a hill back of the town, about 250 yards from the river; built by the English after their conquest of Canada more than 100 years ago. It covered about 2 acres of ground, was quadrangular in shape, with bastions and barracks. It had embankments nearly 20 feet high, a deep, dry ditch, and was surrounded by a double row of pickets.

"The town too was surrounded by strong pickets 14 feet high, with loopholes to shoot through. Those pickets had been erected as defences against the Indians, and were still in good condition. There were in them four strong gates on different streets."

"Then the British couldn't get in to harm the folks, could they, papa?" asked Elsie.

"They would be able to, when they had finished the fortifications they had begun to build on the opposite side of the river," replied the captain; "so General Hull decided that it would be best to cross at once and drive them away.

"It was not easy to find boats enough to take his twenty-two hundred men across, but by great exertion he succeeded in getting enough to carry four hundred at a time, but should the British see them crossing they would in all probability attack that small number before the others could cross to take part in the fight. So Hull resorted to strategy. Toward the evening of the 11th all the boats were sent down the river in full view of the British, while at the same time Colonel M'Arthur with his regiment marched away in the same direction. The British were deceived and made ready to dispute their passage. But after dark troops and boats returned up the river past Detroit to Bloody Bridge, a mile and a half above the town, and made arrangements to cross the river there, which they did."

"Why was it called by that dreadful name—Bloody Bridge, papa?" asked Elsie.

"Because the Indians in Pontiac's time

attacked and killed so many—fifty-nine—of the
English there. Do you not remember my telling you about it?"

"Oh, yes, sir, when we went to Mackinaw
before!" exclaimed the little girl.

"At dawn the regular troops and the Ohio
volunteers crossed over to the Canadian side,
and there hoisted the American flag," continued
the captain.

"But I shall not now go into all the details
of the marching and fighting that followed—
how Hull changed his orders and restrained his
brave, patriotic officers and men from attacks
upon the enemy which they were eager to make,
until they were almost convinced that he was
either a traitor or a coward.

"He was doubtless too old for the command
which had been given him. He had done good
service in the Revolutionary War, and no doubt
was really a patriot still, but he lacked energy,
vigilance, and decision, and was too slow to
take advantage of the necessities and mistakes
of the foe; though he might have done much
better but for the remissness of the Secretary
of War and General Dearborn. His mistakes
and dilatoriness bore very hard upon the brave
fellows under him, who were burning with
patriotic zeal for the discomfiture of the foe,
and he perceived that, though they obeyed

orders, there was a mutinous spirit among them that could scarcely be restrained. Therefore he called a council of field-officers, and by their advice it was agreed to march immediately upon Malden.

"Orders were at once issued for all the needful preparations and received with universal joy by the little army of men longing to defend their country.

"But before these were completed, or the long summer day was quite over, there came another order from the commanding general; an order for the army to recross the river to Detroit—abandoning Canada and its people to the vengeance of the British; leaving unprotected its inhabitants, who, trusting Hull's promised protection, had refused to take up arms for defence against the Americans. That order was in consequence of news which had reached Hull that a considerable force of British regulars, militia, and Indians were coming to attack the little army in the rear."

"Did our soldiers like to go back without fighting the British first, papa?" asked Elsie.

"No, my child, not at all; but they were obedient soldiers, and did as they were ordered by their commander, though sullenly, feeling themselves humiliated by being compelled to act like cowards. During that night and the next morning they crossed the deep, dark river and encamped on the rolling plain back of Fort Detroit.

" Not quite all of them, however. Major Denny, with 130 convalescents, and a corps of artillerists, under Lieutenant Anderson, were left behind in a strong house that had been stockaded and called Fort Gowris. Denny was ordered to defend the post to the last extremity, so long as attacked with only musketry, but to leave it if powerful artillery should be brought against it.

" Hull and his army were in need of supplies, which he knew were being sent him under the command of Captain Brush, who had come as far as the River Raisin, but was detained there by the knowledge that a party of Indians under Tecumseh, with perhaps some British regulars, had crossed the Detroit from Malden and were lying near the mouth of the Huron River, twenty-five miles below Detroit, for the purpose of seizing the men, cattle, provisions, and mail that Captain Brush had in charge.

" Brush had asked Hull to send him an escort. Hull at first flatly refused; but, after much persuasion on the part of his officers, despatched Major Van Horn with a detachment of two hundred men to join Brush and help convoy the cattle, provisions, and mail. The major obeyed promptly, but was not successful; being surprised by the Indians, who lay in ambush and attacked him by the way. The Americans fought gallantly, but lost seventeen killed and several wounded.

"When the news reached the fort Hull was greatly disconcerted. His officers urged him to send a larger force to the aid of Brush—as many as five hundred; but he refused. 'I can spare only one hundred,' he said.

"That, as the officers knew, would not be enough; so, though indignant and alarmed for the safety of Brush and the needed stores he was bringing, they had to give up the hope of helping him for the present.

"But Hull perceived that his troops were angry and felt mutinous, and it was then he called his officers together, and after consulting them gave the orders for preparations to march upon Malden; but, as we have seen, before they could be carried out he changed his mind and ordered the army to cross the river to Detroit. He now felt the need of securing the supplies under Brush and ordered Colonel Miller to take six hundred men, go to that officer's assistance, and escort him to Detroit. Before starting upon their perilous expedition the troops paraded on the north side of Jefferson Avenue, and there Colonel Miller addressed them as they stood in marching order. 'Soldiers,' he said, 'we are going to meet the enemy, and to beat them. The reverse of the 5th (that was Van Horn's) must be repaired. The blood of our brethren, spilled by the savages, must be avenged. I will lead you. You shall not disgrace yourselves or me. Every man who shall leave the ranks or fall back without orders will be instantly put to death. I charge the officers to execute this order.'

"Then turning to the veteran Fourth Regiment of regulars, he said, 'My brave soldiers, you will add another victory to that of Tippecanoe—another laurel to that gained upon the Wabash last fall. If there is now any man in the ranks of the detachment who fears to meet the enemy, let him fall out and stay behind.'

"He paused, and a loud huzza went up from the entire corps, and 'I'll not stay! I'll not stay!' came from every lip.

"Miller led them to the River Rouge that night, and they bivouacked on its southern shore, having crossed it in two scows. Early the next morning they took up their march again, Major Thompson Maxwell, with his spies, leading the way; next a vanguard of forty men under Captain Snelling of the Fourth Regulars, while the infantry marched in two columns, about two hundred yards apart, the cavalry keeping the road in the centre in double file. The artillery followed, with flank guards of riflemen at suitable distances. Marching in that order a line of battle could be formed almost instantly, but it was slow and toilsome work to move the cannon over the marshy ground along which their road lay.

"It was Sunday morning, the weather sultry, the sky overcast with clouds, not a leaf stirring on the trees; in the distance they could see a few fleet Indians hurrying along; but nothing of much consequence occurred until some time in the afternoon, when they were nearing the Indian village of Maguaga, fourteen miles below Detroit. But there a man named White, who had joined them as a new recruit, hurrying on ahead of the rest, was shot from his horse near the cabin of an Indian chief called Walk-in-the-Water, by some Indians concealed behind it, and before the vanguard could reach the spot he was scalped.

"There were oak woods near Maguaga, which Captain Snelling and his regulars reached between three and four o'clock in the afternoon. In the meantime the flying savages the Americans had seen that morning, and who were the scouts of Major Muir, the commander of the Forty-first British regiment, had carried

to him, in his camp at Brownstown, the news
that the Americans, strong in numbers, were
advancing upon them. There were in that
camp 100 regulars, a good many Canadian
militiamen, and between 200 and 300 Indians.
Lossing mentions 4 chiefs of note among those
—Tecumseh, Walk-in-the-Water, Split-log, and
Lame-Hand.

"These troops had been sent over from Fort
Malden by Proctor to repeat their doings of
the ¡5th—when Van Horn was defeated—cut
off communication between Detroit and Captain Brush at the Raisin, and get possession of
the stores he was bringing.

"As soon as Muir and Tecumseh heard the
news brought by the spies they broke up their
camp, hurried on to Maguaga, and formed an
ambush in the Oak Woods, where the trees
and bushes were thick enough to conceal
them. There they watched for the coming
of the Americans and were joined by a
fresh detachment of troops sent by General
Brock.

"Snelling and his soldiers had just entered
the clearing when there came first a single shot,
then the terrific yells of the scores of savages,
followed by a terrible volley from the whole
British line."

"Oh, papa! then did our soldiers turn

round and run back to the others?" asked
little Elsie.

"No, my child, they stood their ground and
returned the fire like the brave men and patriots
they were. Colonel Miller heard the sounds
and he and his men started on the double quick,
came up, and formed in battle order, and as they
did so he waved his sword high over his head,
crying in his clear, loud voice, 'Charge, boys!
charge!' His order was instantly, gallantly,
and effectually obeyed, Lossing tells us, while
at the same time a six-pounder poured in a
storm of grapeshot that harmed the foe not a
little.

"At the same time the Michigan and Ohio
volunteers charged a body of Indians at the left
of the British and near the river, driving them
back, and causing them to flee; and the whites
in the ranks of the enemy, mistaking them for
helpers of the Americans, fired upon them also,
and the Indians returned it. So that our foes
were helping us by fighting among themselves,
and the mistake created such confusion in the
British ranks that they wavered, broke, and
fled, leaving Tecumseh and his Indians to bear
the brunt of the fight.

"Muir rallied his men, in a good position,
but the sound of firing in the woods on their
left alarmed them again, so that they ran

away, got in their boats, and fled across the river to Malden with all possible expedition.

"After a little more fighting the Indians too broke, and Miller ordered Sloan to pursue them. But he seemed to hesitate, and Snelling rushing up to him gave him a peremptory order to dismount, sprang into the saddle himself, and dashed away at the head of his troops, his red hair streaming in the wind, for he had lost his hat in the course of the fight. He pursued the flying foe for more than two miles; then Lieutenant-colonel Miller, realizing the danger of an ambuscade, and that night was approaching, and the wounded needed attention, ordered a suspension of the chase."

"Ah, that was a victory!" exclaimed Walter; "one that ought to have encouraged Hull to defend Detroit; it seems it didn't, though."

"Were there many killed in that battle, papa?" asked Grace.

"Of the Americans 18 were killed and 57 wounded," replied the captain. "The British, according to their account, lost 24 of their regulars, only 1 of whom was killed. They failed to mention how many of the militia and Indians, but our troops found 40 of the Indians dead on the field; how many of the militia, if any, I do not know.

"Miller was anxious to follow up his advan-

tage, to press on to the assistance of Captain
Brush and the getting of his stores to Detroit;
so sent a messenger to Hull to carry the news
of his successful fight with the enemy and ask
for a supply of provisions.

"In response Hull sent Colonel M'Arthur
with 100 men and 600 rations, ordering him to
go down the river in boats to the relief of
Miller and his men. M'Arthur, who seems to
have been always ready and prompt, set out a
little past two in the morning, in nine boats,
and in the darkness and rain passed the British vessels *Queen Charlotte* and *Hunter*, and
reached his destination in safety.

"Then the wounded were at once carried to
the boats to be taken to Detroit. But it was
now daylight, and it was found impossible to
pass the British vessels. Fortunately M'Arthur
had foreseen that difficulty, and ordered wagons
sent down, and now leaving the boats he had
the wounded carried through the woods to the
road, placed in the wagons, and so taken the
rest of the way to their destination."

"But what did he do with the boats, papa?"
asked Elsie.

"The British took them," replied her father.
"Colonel Cass had gone down and tried to
secure them, but the enemy had already got
possession.

"Miller had been thrown from his horse during the fight, and was too much injured to press on immediately to the River Raisin. He sent a messenger to Hull, and Cass met him on his way. He knew that time was precious, that Proctor would be likely to send a larger force to prevent our men from reaching Brush, and attack him himself. Therefore Cass wanted to take Miller's place and hurry on with the detachment to Brush's assistance, so he sent a laconic despatch to General Hull: 'Sir, Colonel Miller is sick; may I relieve him?—L. Cass.' No reply came, and he returned to Detroit, meeting on the way an express taking positive orders to Miller for him and his troops to return to headquarters.

"Miller and his men were only twenty-two miles from the Raisin, and were sorely disappointed by this order, but obeyed it, leaving their camp at noon on the day after the battle, and going slowly back to Detroit."

"Oh, I do think that was too bad!" exclaimed Lucilla. "I don't think I could have obeyed such a man as Hull."

"It would have been even worse than rendering obedience to Captain Raymond has sometimes proved, eh?" her father said, with a humorous look and smile.

"Oh, ten thousand times, papa, dear!" she

answered earnestly. "Haven't you found out that for years it has been—almost always just a pleasure to me to obey you?"

"It is long since I have felt at all doubtful of that, daughter," he returned, in tender tones.

CHAPTER VI.

For a moment Captain Raymond seemed lost in thought. It was a question from his daughter Elsie that caused him to resume the thread of his narrative.

"Papa," she asked, "had the British got their guns all ready to fire at the Americans when Colonel Miller and his men got back to Detroit? and did they begin at once?"

"No; the British were still busy with their preparations, with which General Hull did not seem disposed to interfere; and it was hard indeed for his brave, patriotic officers to obey his orders to refrain from doing so. They began to think he was either a traitor or an imbecile, and by no means fit to have the command. They consulted together, and concluded that salvation for the little army could be secured only by depriving him of the command and giving it to another. Miller was asked to take it, but declined and proposed M'Arthur, who was the senior officer of the volunteers and one of the most vigilant, active, and energetic men in the service.

"But when it came to carrying out their

plans they hesitated to take so bold a step. Relief might come soon from Ohio, Governor Meigs accompany it in person, and then the honor could be properly tendered him. Colonel Cass acted promptly upon that suggestion, writing to the governor a very strong and urgent appeal for help to be forwarded with all haste; telling him that the army was in a very critical situation 'from causes not fit to be put on paper'; that Malden might easily have been reduced, but the golden opportunity had been allowed to pass unimproved. He asked for, at least, two thousand men, and that the governor would accompany them.

"But before this letter had been shown to the other officers the British were collecting in force at Sandwich, and Cass added a postscript. 'Since the other side of this letter was written, new circumstances have arisen. The British force is opposite, and our situation had nearly reached its crisis. Believe all the bearer will tell you. Believe it, however it may astonish you, as much as if told by one of us. Even a c—— is talked of by e——. The bearer will supply the vacancy. On you we depend.' The first blank meant a capitulation, the second commanding general."

"But why didn't he say what he meant, papa?" asked Elsie.

"Because there was danger of the letter falling into the hands of the wrong person. It was signed by Cass, Finley, M'Arthur, Taylor, and Colonel Elijah Brush, of the Michigan militia."

"Was Major Denny still on the Canadian side, captain?" asked Evelyn.

"No; he had evacuated Fort Gowris and crossed the river to Detroit. On his doing so the British under Captain Dixon of the Royal Engineers immediately took possession and planted a battery so as to command Detroit. The American artillery begged leave from Hull to open upon them from the fort with twenty-four pounders, but were forbidden, and the enemy was allowed to go on unmolested with his preparations to fire upon Detroit."

"Well!" exclaimed Lucilla, "I'm sure that looked as if he was in league with his country's foes; unless he had lost his reason."

"Yes," said her father, "yet I do not doubt his patriotism or his intention to do what he deemed best under the circumstances; but he was timid, and as I have said before, did not receive the help and encouragement he had a right to expect from the Secretary of War or General Dearborn, who failed to inform him of the armistice, which would have enabled him to wait for the arrival of needed provisions and reinforcements. And he was too honest himself to suspect the deceptions the British practised upon him—dressing raw militiamen in uniform and mixing them in with their regulars, sending a letter to be intercepted by him, threatening a descent of five thousand Indians from Mackinaw. But I think he owed it to the officers under him to consult with them; which he did not do."

"Had the British got Captain Brush with the soldiers and provisions, papa?" asked Elsie.

"No, he was still in the same place, waiting for reinforcements to enable him to reach Detroit; and on the 14th Hull sent him word that he could not spare a large enough detachment to escort him, and that he might either stay where he was till further orders, or take a roundabout course to avoid the enemy. But after the men had gone with the letter Hull again changed his mind and sent M'Arthur and Cass with 350 men to escort Brush, who was supposed to be not more than 12 miles away.

"They took a circuitous route, got entangled in a swamp, and could not go on. They were without provisions, tired and hungry, and were just preparing to bivouac for the night—for the evening twilight was fading away—when a courier came with an order from Hull for them to return immediately to Detroit. They obeyed and arrived there about ten o'clock the next morning.

"At a little past noon of that day General Brock sent two of his officers with a flag to bear a summons to General Hull for the unconditional surrender of the post. 'The force at my disposal,' he said, 'authorizes me to require of you the surrender of Detroit. It is far from my inclination to join in a war of extermination, but you must be aware that the numerous body of Indians who have attached themselves to my troops will be beyond my control the moment the contest commences.'"

"And Hull meekly surrendered without any more ado?" said Lucilla, in a tone between assertion and enquiry.

"No, not yet," replied her father. "Poor man! really patriotic and proud, he no doubt felt sorely tried and humiliated at the very thought of surrender to his country's foes; at the same time, being ignorant of the armistice and not knowing when succor would arrive, having only a thousand men in fighting condition, his force wasting with disease, disappointment, and death, it seemed to him very uncertain whether he could keep the foe at bay till help would come; but his troops were eager to measure strength with the enemy, and confident in their ability to do so successfully.

"So difficult did Hull find it to decide what was the best and wisest course of conduct that he kept the flag waiting two hours; but at last he said to Brock's messengers that he had no other reply to make than that he was ready to meet any force at his disposal, and any consequence that might result.

"His own troops were greatly pleased when they learned what his answer to Brock had been. They watched the return of the flag, and when it reached the Canadian shore the bearers were startled by a loud huzza from the American fort and camp. Our brave soldiers believed and rejoiced in the thought that the time for action had come, or was near at hand; they were confident of victory, and at once set about the most active preparations for the fight.

"Jesup, serving as adjutant-general to Hull, rode down to Spring Wells to reconnoitre the enemy at Sandwich. He saw that the British vessel, *Queen Charlotte*, had taken such a position that she could cover the landing of the enemy there with her guns. He thought a battery might be used to drive her away, so selecting a suitable spot for it, he hastened back to Detroit, told Hull what he proposed to do, and asked him to send down a twenty-pounder.

"Hull refused and Jesup rode back to the spot he wished to defend, to find Snelling there with a few men and a six-pounder, occupying the very place he had selected. By the way, it is said that Snelling was to have been married that evening to a daughter of Colonel Thomas Hunt, and that when about to leave the fort for Spring Wells, he asked of Hull, 'If I drive the redcoats back, may I return and be married?" and that General Hull consented, and the marriage took place that same evening.

"When Detroit was surrendered Snelling refused to raise the white flag, and when marched as a prisoner through the streets of Montreal, being ordered by a British officer to take off his cap to Nelson's monument, he refused and kept it on in spite of the efforts of the soldiers to enforce the order, and finally General Brock ordered them to respect the scruples of a brave man."

"I respect and like Brock for that," said Walter. "He was a far better, braver, nobler man than Proctor."

"He was indeed!" assented the captain. "Cruelty and cowardice usually go hand in hand, and they were both prominent traits in Proctor's character. But to return. Both Snelling and Jesup, perceiving that the greater part of the British force was at Sandwich, hastened back to Hull, and, reporting that fact to him, Jesup asked for 150 men to go over and spike the enemy's guns opposite Detroit. Hull said he could not spare so many. 'Give me one hundred, then,' entreated Jesup. 'Only one hundred,' added Snelling imploringly. Hull only replied that he would consider it, and then took refuge in the fort; for at four o'clock the British battery, whose guns Snelling and Jesup had proposed to spike, began firing shot and shell upon the fort, the town, and the camp. Then all the troops except Finley's regiment, which was stationed three hundred yards northwest of the fort, were ordered within the walls, crowding it far too much for comfort."

The captain paused, and Grandma Elsie remarked that she remembered reading of some interesting occurrences given by Lossing in notes to his history of the attack upon Detroit and its fort.

"One was that during the evening a large shell fell upon the roof of a private dwelling, two stories high, and coming down through the roof and upper floor, fell upon the table around which the family were sitting, then through to the cellar, and they had just time to fly from the house when the shell exploded, tearing it to pieces."

"That was a very narrow escape for them," remarked Violet.

"Please tell us some more, grandma," begged Neddie, and Grandma Elsie kindly continued.

"There was a battery commanded by a brave soldier—Lieutenant Daliba," she said. "He stood on the ramparts during the cannonade, and when he saw the smoke or flash of the enemy's cannon he would call out to his men, 'Down!' and they would drop behind the parapet until the ball had struck.

"Near the battery was a large pear-tree which was somewhat in the way, and Colonel Mack, of the Michigan militia, ordered a young volunteer named John Miller to cut it down. He made haste to obey, seizing an axe and falling vigorously to work; but when he had cut about halfway through the trunk one of the enemy's balls struck it and nearly finished the work. The young man turned coolly toward the British and called out, 'Send us another, John Bull; you can cut faster than I can.'"

"Was the British soldier that fired it named John Bull?" queried Neddie.

"Why, that's what we call Englishmen, don't you know?" said his sister Elsie. "And we are all Brother Jonathans. Aren't we, papa?"

"That's what they call us," returned her

father, with a smile, "and though not a very euphonious name, I, for one, prefer it to John Bull."

"So do I," she said.

"But Jonathan's a boy's name," objected Ned sturdily. "Men and boys can be Jonathans, but women and girls can't."

"Well, I don't want to be," said Elsie. "It isn't a pretty name; but John Bull's worse. Grandma, haven't you another little story to tell us?"

"One more, which I found in Lossing's book," replied Grandma Elsie pleasantly. "He says it is related that while cannonading was going on, the shot striking thick and fast around the fort, a negro was seen on its roof. He stood near a chimney, watching the firing of the British on the other side of the river, and whenever he saw the smoke of a cannon would spring behind the chimney till the shot had struck, then peep out again.

"At length one struck the top of the chimney just over his head, tore it to pieces, and covered him with brick and mortar. He jumped aside, shaking himself free, as well as he might, from the dust and rubbish, and exclaiming: 'What de debble you doin' up dar?' then hastened away to find a safer spot."

"Wasn't that a bad, swearing word, grandma?" queried Ned.

"It was not a nice word," she answered. "I should be sorry indeed to hear it used by my sons or grandsons."

"My papa never says such words, nor Maxie, nor any of my relations, and I don't mean ever, ever to say them," said the little fellow, looking up into his father's face.

"No, my son, I trust you never shall," returned the captain gravely, laying a hand affectionately on the child's head.

"Please tell the rest, papa," pleaded little Elsie, and her father resumed the thread of his narrative.

"The British kept up their bombardment until near midnight, our men returning it with great spirit and disabling two of the enemy's guns. About twilight someone proposed that as the fort did not command the river, a strong battery should be placed near the margin of the river and used in destroying the foe when they attempted to land. A suitable place for the purpose was chosen, but Hull utterly refused to allow the plan to be carried out; and in the early twilight of the next morning—a beautiful Sunday morning—they were allowed to cross without the least attempt being made to hinder them.

"Six hundred Indians, commanded by two British colonels and Tecumseh, had crossed the

night before and taken position in the woods
to attack the Americans in flank and rear should
they attempt to hinder the landing of the British regulars and militia, 770 strong with 5
pieces of light artillery.

"They all breakfasted, then moved upon the
fort—the whites in a single column, their left
flank covered by the Indians, a mile and a half
distant in the woods; their right resting on
the Detroit River, defended by the *Queen
Charlotte.*

"Colonel Miller, with the Fourth Regiment,
was now in the fort; the Ohio volunteers with
part of the Michigan militia were posted behind the town palisades, to annoy the enemy's
whole left flank. The rest of the militia were
stationed in the upper part of the town to keep
back the Indians, who had joined the British in
order to be permitted to plunder and kill the
American whites.

"Our men were waiting, watching the cautiously approaching foe, eager to fire upon them
the moment they were in the best position to
receive the most destructive onslaught—for
wives, children, and feeble aged ones were in
danger of becoming victims to their inhuman
thirst for blood and plunder, and that foe had
reached a point within five hundred yards of
their line when there came a peremptory com-

mand from General Hull for them to retreat
within the fort.

"The soldiers were very angry but obeyed,
while the enemy drew nearer and prepared to
storm the fort. The shot were coming thick
and fast now from the Canadian shore. A ball
came bounding over the wall of the fort and
struck a group standing before one of the officer's quarters, killing two officers and a surgeon and badly wounding another. The next
moment two other soldiers on the inside of the
fort and two on the outside were killed.

"There were women and children in the
house where the officers were killed, among
them General Hull's daughter and her children.
Some of the women were bespattered with the
blood of the slain, and almost paralyzed with
fear; some were carried senseless to the bomb-
proof vault for safety.

"The general saw the effect of the ball from
a distance, and did not know whether his own
child was killed or not.

"Just then an officer of the Michigan militia
in the town came to ask if they alone were to
defend it, as he had seen the approach of the
enemy without a gun being fired from the fort
or the twenty-four pounders outside; also to
inform Hull that the Indians were at the tan-
yard, close upon the town. Hull did not

answer his queries, but stepped into a room in the barracks, hastily wrote a note, and handing it to his son, Captain Hull, directed him to display a white flag immediately from the walls of the fort, where it might be seen by the British Captain Dixon, over the river.

"The order was promptly obeyed. The flag was a tablecloth. By order of General Hull it was waved from one of the bastions by Captain Burton, of the Fourth Regiment.

"The firing soon ceased, and in a few minutes Captain Hull was seen leaving the fort with a flag of truce. At the same time a boat was despatched across the river to Captain Dixon, commander of the battery on the Canada shore.

"General Hull was acting without consultation with any of his officers, and no one knew what were his intentions, but the sight of the white flag upon the walls awakened painful suspicions, and presently the arrival of two British officers, Colonel M'Donell and Major Glegg, made it evident that the garrison was betrayed.

"Hull had acted entirely on his own responsibility, consulting no one, and this quick surrender, without a single shot having been fired upon the enemy, or an effort made to stay his course, was almost as unexpected and unwelcome to the brave, patriotic men under him as

a thunderbolt out of a clear sky. So angry
and indignant were they that for a moment
nothing but reverence for gray hairs and venera-
tion for a soldier of the Revolution, who had
served his country well in that war, saved him
from personal violence at their hands; it is said
that many of them shed tears of mortification
and disappointment.

"The terms of capitulation were soon settled,
and Hull issued a general order to his troops,
stating that with pain and anxiety he announced
to the Northwest Army that a sense of duty
had compelled him to agree to articles of
capitulation which he then enumerated.

"You will remember that he had sent Colonels
M'Arthur and Cass toward the River Raisin,
then ordered them back; they were coming,
but had not yet arrived; he sent a messenger to
meet them, with a note to M'Arthur informing
him of the surrender, and that he and his command were included in it, as prisoners of war.
They had drawn near enough to Detroit to see
the white flags that had silenced the British
cannon, reaching there thoroughly exhausted
with marching and hunger—for Hull had sent
them off without provisions and failed to keep
his promise to send some after them; so that
for forty-eight hours they had nothing to eat
but some green pumpkins and potatoes they

had found in the fields. As they went and came they had been observing the enemy, taking note of his numbers and movements, and concluded that they might easily capture him by falling upon his rear while the army at Detroit attacked him in front. But what did the silence mean? The armies were within half cannon shot of each other, but there was no firing; both seemed silent as the grave, from where these listeners stood. Had there been any evidence of fighting, M'Arthur would have fallen upon the rear of the foe, without waiting for orders.

"But Hull's courier was seen approaching, and in a few moments more these patriots heard the almost unbearable tidings that Hull had given them up to the foe without an effort at self-defence.

"M'Arthur tried to communicate with Hull, but failed. He sent Hull's note to Captain Brush, with a message from himself, 'By the within letter you will see that the army under General Hull has been surrendered. By the articles you will see that provision has been made for your command; you will, therefore, I hope, return to Ohio with us.'

"Lossing tells us in a note that Captain Elliott, the son of Colonel Elliott, with a Frenchman and Wyandot Indian, arrived at Brush's camp on the Raisin, bearing a flag of truce, a copy of the capitulation at Detroit, and authority to receive the surrender of Brush and his men.

"A lieutenant, the officer of the day, blind-folded Elliott and led him to the block-house. Brush, when informed of Elliott's arrival and on what errand, doubting his authority, had him arrested and placed in confinement. On reading M'Arthur's letter, however, he learned his mistake; but instead of releasing Elliott at once and complying with Hull's order, he hastily packed up the public property at the Raisin, and with his whole command and his cattle, started for Ohio, leaving orders that Elliott should be kept in confinement until the next day. Elliott was very angry, and sent for Tecumseh to pursue Brush; but it was too late."

"Did M'Arthur do that way too, papa?" asked little Elsie.

"No; when on the evening of the 17th Colonel Elliott came with authority from Brock to receive tokens of the submission of M'Arthur's detachment, the dark eyes of that officer flashed with indignation, then filled with tears of mortification; he thrust his sword into the ground and broke it to pieces, then tore his epaulets from his shoulders. But having in

that way relieved his feelings, he became calm
and dignified, while in the dim twilight, Cass
and their whole detachment were marched
into the fort and stacked their arms."

"Oh, how hard it must have been for
M'Arthur, and all of them, indeed!" exclaimed
Lucilla.

"Were they shut up in jail, papa?" asked
Elsie.

"The volunteers and militia with some of the
regular officers, not of high rank, were paroled
and allowed to go home," replied her father.
"Those belonging to Michigan were discharged
right there, the Ohioans sent in a vessel to
Cleveland, and there relieved from British control. General Hull and the regulars were held
as prisoners of war and sent to Montreal."

"But that wasn't the worst for poor General
Hull, was it, papa?" said Grace. "The blame
he got from the whole country, and being tried
for cowardice, condemned to be shot, and all the
rest of it, I should think, must have been far
worse. Do you think he was really a coward
and so very much to blame, papa?"

"No," replied her father; "he was perhaps
weak, but neither wicked nor cowardly; he
was very cautious, prudent, and anxious to
save the women, children, and aged men in the
fort from falling into the hands of the blood-

thirsty, tomahawking, scalping savages. Had
he known of the armistice and that provisions
and ammunition were coming, and had Dearborn and the Secretary of War done their duty,
the result might have been very different. As
it was, he was made the scapegoat for all."

"Poor man! I feel sorry for him," sighed
Grace.

"As I do," said her father. "I have no
doubt he did what he believed to be his duty
as a humane and Christian man. In parting at
Detroit with one of his aids he said to him,
'God bless you, my young friend! You return
to your family without a stain; as for myself,
I have sacrificed a reputation dearer to me than
life, but I have saved the inhabitants of Detroit,
and my heart approves the act.' In his despatch to the Secretary of War he generously
said, 'I well know the responsibility of the
measure, and take the whole of it on myself.'
And after alluding to M'Arthur, Finley, Miller,
and Cass in commendatory terms, he adds, 'If
aught has taken place during the campaign
which is honorable to the army, these officers
are entitled to a large share of it. If the last
act should be disapproved, no part of the censure belongs to them.'"

"That was noble and generous!" exclaimed
Evelyn, with warmth, "and it was shameful,

shameful that all the blame was put upon him
when Dearborn and the Government were really
so very much more deserving of it."

"Yes," said Grandma Elsie, in her own sweet,
gentle tones, "and he bore it in such a patient,
Christian spirit; confident that his countrymen
would some day understand and do him justice.
I have read that on his deathbed he was asked
whether he still believed he had done right in
surrendering Detroit, and he answered that he
did and was thankful he had been enabled to
do it."

"I suppose," said Evelyn, "it was a great
mistake, but he acted as he deemed best for
others and that at a great sacrifice of himself;
so I think he was a noble, generous man,
worthy of all honor, and I am very glad he was
not made to suffer death, though I am not sure
that what he had to bear was not worse."

"Yes," exclaimed Walter, "and how I de-
spise those mean fellows who put all the blame
on him when they themselves deserved a great
deal more of it than he!"

"How long did the British keep possession
of Detroit, papa?" asked Grace.

"Until Perry's victory on Lake Erie restored
it to the Americans."

"Oh, that was a grand victory!" exclaimed
Lucilla, with enthusiasm.

"Yes; the navy did well in that war," the captain said, with a smile and a sparkle in his eye. "I have always felt a patriotic pride in the achievements of Perry, McDonough, and Isaac Hull. The first two were earnest Christian men and gave all the glory to God. I do not know, but hope the gallant Hull was a Christian also."

CHAPTER VII.

THE *Dolphin* reached Detroit that evening, did not stop, but slowly passed the city, which extends six or seven miles along the river, then on down the stream, the captain pointing out historical scenes, now on this side now on that.

They were already on Lake Erie before the older ones retired for the night, passed Put-In-Bay and discussed with interest Perry's victory of September 10, 1813, though, as all were familiar with the details of the famous contest and triumph for the little American navy, the story was not repeated.

"How many islands are there in the group, papa?" Grace asked, as they neared them; "and to which State do they belong?"

"There are ten," he said, "and they are a part of Ottawa township, Ohio. The group takes its name from the largest one, which contains about two thousand acres. You can see there is a beautiful bay on this north side: that is Put-In-Bay—it is what gives the name to the island and is celebrated as the place where Captain Perry with his little United States fleet

on Lake Erie, in the last war with Great
Britain, of which we have been talking so much
in the last few days, waited for the coming of
her fleet, and whence he sailed out to meet and
conquer it.

"It required great address and vigilance to
make his little squadron ready and get it into the
lake, but spite of illness, head winds, and being
narrowly watched by the foe, he got safely out
upon the lake just as the British squadron hove
in sight."

"Perry had difficulty in getting his vessels
over the bar, had he not, sir?" asked Walter.

"Yes; it was done by the use of camels; a
very difficult operation."

"Camels, papa?" exclaimed Grace, with a
puzzled look.

"Yes, daughter; not the camels of the desert,
however," returned the captain, giving her a
slightly amused smile.

"Nautical camels are hollow cases of wood,
made in two halves, so as to embrace the keel
and lay hold of the hull of a ship on both sides.
Those cases are first filled with water and sunk,
in order to be fixed on. The water is then
pumped out, and while that is being done the
vessel gradually rises; and that process is
continued till at length it passes over the
shoal."

"Perry must certainly have been a very persevering and energetic man," remarked Mrs.
Travilla.

"He certainly was all that and more," returned the captain; "a brave, patriotic, Christian man. It has been truly said that the courage with which the *Lawrence* was defended
has been hardly, if ever, surpassed; and that
his real claim to fame rests less on his actual
victory than on the pluck, energy, and readiness
to adapt himself to circumstances, which he
showed in the preparation of the two brigs and
getting them and the other vessels out in the
lake, collecting sailors, etc. But it is singular
that the American public have always made so
much more of his victory over an inferior force,
than of McDonough's on Lake Champlain,
which was won against decided odds in vessels,
men, and metal."

"Oh, papa!" cried Lucilla, in a slightly
reproachful tone, "you are really the last person I should have expected to try to belittle
Perry's hard-won victory."

"My child, I am not doing that," returned
her father in gentle, reproving accents. "I
would not have Perry's fame lessened, but
McDonough's increased."

"Excuse me, papa dear, I might have known
that," she responded penitently.

"What is the name of that little island lying at the mouth of the bay, captain?" queried Evelyn.

"Gibraltar," he replied; "it is picturesque and rocky, and on it stands the monument commemorating the victory and its heroes."

"I should like to visit the island one of these days," said Grace.

"I hope to give you that pleasure at some future time," her father said; "but now it is growing so late in the season that we must hasten on our way if we would make even a flying visit to other and more interesting and important points. The islands are worth visiting; the scenery is lovely, and there is excellent boating, also fishing, in the clear, shallow waters of the bay and lake."

"All that sounds quite appetizing," said Voilet. "I think we might be able to pass some days or weeks there very delightfully when not hurried for time."

"There are a great many fine grapes raised here, are there not?" asked Evelyn.

"Yes; grape growing and wine making are the principal industries; the climate and soil being better suited to them than is any other in the Union; or rather, I should say, on the Atlantic slope. Another item of interest is a cave of considerable dimensions."

"Papa," asked Grace, "how long did that battle of Lake Erie last?"

"Three hours and a quarter. It was a sanguinary fight, ending in a splendid victory for Perry, who was about twenty-seven years old, and had never before borne part in a naval engagement."

"Yes, it was sanguinary; the carnage was terrible," said Mr. Dinsmore. "What harrowing scenes there must have been!"

"Some comical ones, too," remarked Walter, with a chuckle. "I have read somewhere that Perry's first lieutenant, Yarnall, came to him during the fight and told him that all the officers of the first division were either killed or wounded. I don't know that he mentioned himself among them, but it was very evident that he had been hurt, for his face was covered with blood from a wound in his forehead, his nose dreadfully swollen by a blow from a splinter, and there was another wound in his neck."

"He must have been a brave and persevering fellow to go on fighting with all those hurts," said Grace. "But what was it he wanted of Perry?"

"More men to help with his part of the fight; and Perry let him have them. But soon he came back on the same errand, and that time

Perry had to refuse. 'You must make out by yourself; I have no more to furnish you,' he said. And now he could not help smiling at Yarnall's appearance, for in addition to his swelled nose and the blood on his face he was covered with cattails from the hammock mattresses that had been struck and torn by the enemy's balls; they were sticking all over his face and gave him much the aspect of a great owl. When he went below after the fight was over, even the wounded men had to laugh at his comical and hideous appearance."

"I remember reading of the narrow escape that fell to the lot of the second lieutenant," said Rosie, when Walter had finished his little anecdote, "he was standing close beside Perry, fighting his division, when a grape-shot struck him in the breast, and he fell. Perry lifted him up, and as there was no wound to be seen, told him to rally, for he could not be hurt. He was only stunned into momentary unconsciousness, and when able to speak, said, pulling out the shot, which had lodged in his waistcoat, 'No, sir! I'm not hurt, but this is my shot.'"

"Yes," said Captain Raymond, "more than one man was shot and killed while speaking to Perry. One was the captain of the gun whose tackle had been shot away. Perry stepped nearer to him to see what was the matter. 'I

can fire, sir,' the sailor said, and was in the
very act of doing so when a twenty-four-pound
shot struck him, passed through his body, and
he fell dead at Perry's feet."

"But Perry escaped unwounded, though
freely exposing himself to danger when necessary for the performance of duty," remarked
Grandma Elsie.   "I have read that he said that
he believed his wife's prayers had saved him;
I have no doubt that his mother's helped him,
for I have read that she was a Christian woman,
and had brought him up in the fear of the Lord.
His young brother too—only twelve years old—
escaped wonderfully, shots passing through his
clothes and hat, a hammock torn from its
fastenings by a ball knocking him down, and
yet no wound being made."

"Lieutenant John Brooks, a handsome young
fellow, was another officer shot while speaking
to Perry," said Captain Raymond, "struck in
the thigh by a cannon ball that drove him some
distance.   It was a terribly painful wound, so
that he shrieked with agony, and besought
Perry to shoot him dead.   Perry ordered him
carried below, and while that was being done
a mulatto boy, his servant, rolled on the deck,
crying out that his master was killed.   He
had been acting as powder boy, and being
ordered to return to his duty did so with the

tears rolling down his cheeks all the time at the thought of his master's suffering!"

There was a moment of silence, broken by Grace.

"Oh, what a dreadful thing war is!" she sighed. "I hope we will never have another. I think nothing could be worse."

"How about submission to despotism, Gracie?" asked Walter. "What sort of condition would this country be in now had not our ancestors waged those two wars with Great Britain?"

"Oh, yes! they were right on the side of America, dreadful as they were," she acknowledged, "the choice being between fighting for freedom or enduring unbearable oppression."

"That is true," he said; "better death than slavery; and had we tamely submitted, instead of resisting as we did, we could never have become the strong, free people that we are."

"And we may well, even yet, thank God for Perry's victory," said the captain; "it led to the immediate evacuation of Detroit and the release of the whole of Michigan Territory from British sway, with all the horrors of Indian atrocities, murder, scalping, and fire. Also it wiped away the disgrace of Hull's ignominious surrender of Detroit, strengthened the hands of the Government, and gave great encouragement to General Harrison and his brave and patriotic soldiers; indeed, to all who were fighting for our country on both land and sea. Harrison had completed his arrangements for invading Canada, and Perry's vessels were used in carrying his army there. That is, the *Niagara* and the lighter vessels of both squadrons.

"One of the measures Harrison had taken for raising the needed complement of troops had been a call upon Governor Shelby of Kentucky, for fifteen hundred men, accompanied by the generous offer to yield the chief command to him, Shelby to be the guiding head and Harrison himself the hand.

"Shelby was one of those who had battled for his country in the days of the Revolution; one of the leaders of the militia who defeated the banded Tories under Major Ferguson on King's Mountain, South Carolina, on the 7th of October, 1781. His valor was conspicuous on that occasion, and he had since been familiarly styled Old King's Mountain."

"A very old man in 1813, I suppose," said Grace.

"Sixty-three," replied her father. "In these days we would hardly consider a man of that age extremely old, though certainly not young. Young enough, however, for Harrison's invitation to rouse his martial spirit to such an extent that he resolved to lead, instead of sending his men against the enemies of his country. He called for mounted volunteers to assemble at Newport, opposite Cincinnati, at the close of July, promising to meet them there in person, lead them to the field of battle, and share with them the dangers and honors of the campaign.

"That call seemed to electrify the people of Kentucky. Young men and veterans vied with each other in enthusiasm, exchanging urgent calls to rally to the defence of their country, for Old King's Mountain would certainly lead them to victory. Twice the required number of men flocked to his standard, and, including Colonel R. M. Johnson's troop, he led 3500 in the direction of Lake Erie.

"On the 12th of September he reached Upper Sandusky, from there he pushed forward with his staff, and on the way heard the glad tidings of Perry's victory. He despatched a courier with the news to Major-General Henry, whom he had left in command of his troops, bidding him hasten forward with them.

"They, and the whole country as well, were greatly inspirited, filled with joy and exultation by the glad tidings; for that victory relieved the whole region of the most gloomy forebodings of evil, leading, as it did, to the destruction of the Indian confederacy, which, in conjunction with the British military power, had been the cause of so much awful suffering and loss to men, women, and children suffering by fire, sword, tomahawk, and scalping knife, and removing the stigma of the surrender of Detroit.

"That victory was one of the most important events of the war, opening the way for Harrison's army to penetrate into Canada and to our repossession of the territory of Michigan. Also removing all doubts of the ability of the Americans to maintain the mastery of the great lakes.

"A poet of the time concluded an epic with these lines:

" 'And though Britons may brag of their ruling the ocean,
And that sort of thing, by the Lord I've a notion—
I'll bet all I'm worth, who takes it ?—who takes ?
Though they're lords of the sea, we'll be lords of the lakes.'

"Well, to go on with my story, by the 16th the whole army of the Northwest, except the troops garrisoning Fort Meigs and minor posts, were on the borders of Lake Erie. Shelby arrived there on the 14th, only a few minutes before a part of Perry's squadron came in, bringing three hundred British prisoners. A few days later they were marched to Chillicothe and Franklinton, escorted by a guard of Kentucky militia.

"And now Harrison made preparations to embark his army. Colonel Johnson was directed to remain at Fort Meigs with his mounted regiment till the expedition should sail, then march toward Detroit, keeping as nearly as possible abreast of the army on the transports, and General M'Arthur, at that time in command of Fort Meigs, was directed to embark artillery, provisions, and stores from that post, and march the regulars there, with Clay's Kentuckians, to the Portage.

"It was on a delightful day, the 20th of September, that the army embarked. On the 24th they rendezvoused on Put-in-Bay Island, and the next day were on the Middle Sisters, five thousand men encamping on its six or seven acres."

"A good many horses besides, I presume," remarked Walter.

"No," said the captain, "the Kentuckians left their horses on the peninsula and were acting as infantry.

"On that day General Harrison and Perry sailed in the *Ariel* to reconnoitre the enemy at Malden. They were entirely successful, and returned at sunset. An order was issued that evening, giving directions for the embarking of the troop, stating the place and manner of landing, the order of march, the attack upon the enemy, and other particulars.

"The order, signed by General E. P. Gaines, exhorted his brave troops to remember that they were the sons of sires whose fame was immortal; that they were to fight for the rights of their insulted country, while their opponents would combat for the unjust pretensions of a master. 'Kentuckians,' he said, 'remember the River Raisin, but remember it only while victory is suspended. The revenge of a soldier cannot be satisfied upon a fallen enemy.'

"It was on a lovely autumnal day, September 27, that the expedition finally set sail, in sixteen armed vessels and almost one hundred boats. They were all in motion at nine o'clock, going northward toward the hostile shore, and then Harrison's stirring address was read to the men on each vessel. At its conclusion there went up a hearty shout for 'Harrison and victory'; then all moved on silently into the Detroit River. Lossing tells us the spectacle was beautiful and sublime.

"The landing place selected by Harrison and Perry was Hartley's Point, opposite the lower end of Bois Blanc Island, and three or four miles below Malden. A low, sandy beach stretched out in front of high sand drifts,

behind which the enemy were supposed to be
lying in wait, and our troops landed in battle
order—Kentucky volunteers on the right,
regulars on the left, Ball's Legion and the
friendly Indians in the centre.

"But no enemy was there. The cowardly
Proctor, in spite of the indignant remonstrances
of Tecumseh, had fled northward with his army
and all he could take with him; leaving Fort
Malden, the storehouses, and navy buildings
smoking ruins. Beside that, he had seized all
the horses of the people of the neighborhood to
help him in his flight."

"The poor people! poor, abused creatures!"
exclaimed Grace, adding, "and probably they
were much frightened lest the Americans
should treat them still worse."

"If so, their fears were soon relieved,"
replied her father; "for as our troops drew
near the town, Governor Shelby in advance,
they were met by a troop of modest, well-
dressed women, who came to implore mercy
and protection. The kind-hearted general soon
calmed their fears.

"The army moved on and entered Malden
with the band playing 'Yankee Doodle.' They
learned that the enemy's rear guard had not
been gone an hour, and Colonel Ball at once
sent an officer and twenty men of his cavalry

after them to prevent the destruction of a bridge over the Tarontee. They were just in time to save it, driving the incendiaries off with a single volley.

"The next morning Harrison crossed it with all his army, excepting a regiment of riflemen left at Amherstburg. At two o'clock on the 29th they entered Sandwich, and the American flotilla reached Detroit, which, you will remember, is opposite, on the western side of the river of the same name. The next day Colonel Johnson and his mounted regiment arrived there."

"Were not the British still in possession of Detroit, papa?" asked Lucilla.

"No; M'Arthur, with seven hundred effective men, had crossed over shortly before and retaken the town, driving off a body of Indians who were hovering about it. Also General Harrison had, to the great joy of the inhabitants, declared Proctor's proclamation of martial law null and void, and the civil government of Michigan restored.

"On Johnson's arrival he received an order from Harrison to cross the river at once with his troops, as he (Harrison) was resolved to push on after the enemy as rapidly as possible. There were two roads, either of which might be taken in the pursuit—by land in the rear of the British, or by Lake Erie to Long Point, and thence across the country. Harrison called a council of his general officers to consider the question, and it was decided to take the land route.

"It was said that Proctor was encamped near Chatham on the Thames; so that was the place for which the whole army of the Americans, except M'Arthur's brigade, left at Detroit, and Ball's and Cass', left at Sandwich, marched on the morning of October 2.

"Two days before that Perry had learned that some small vessels carrying the artillery and baggage of the British had gone up Lake St. Clair toward the Thames. He sent some of his vessels in pursuit, followed them in the *Ariel*, accompanied by the *Caledonia*, and on the day that Harrison left Sandwich the whole of the little squadron appeared off the mouth of the Thames with the provisions, baggage, and amumnition wagons of the American army."

"Had he taken the enemy's vessels?" asked Evelyn.

"No," replied the captain; "they had too much the start of his, and escaped up the Thames. It is said that when the army reached the mouth of that river an eagle was seen hovering above it; and that Harrison remarked to

those about him that it was a presage of success, and Perry, who had landed and was with
the general, added the information that an
eagle was seen hovering over his little squadron on the morning of the 10th of September."

"The day when he fought his naval battle,"
remarked Grace. "Don't you suppose, papa,
this eagle may have been the very same?"

"I think it quite likely," was the reply.

"And it reminds me of the young gamecock
that flew upon a gun-slide on the *Saratoga*,
McDonough's flagship, early in the naval battle
of Plattsburg, clapped his wings and crowed
so lustily and defiantly," said Walter.

"And me of 'Old Abe,' the eagle present in
so many battles of the Civil War," said his
sister Rose. "But please go on with your
story of the battle of the Thames."

"To go back to the morning of October 2,
when Harrison and his troops left Sandwich,"
continued the captain. "We are told that
they pushed on rapidly for 20 miles along the
border of the lake, there came upon 7 British
deserters who told the general that Proctor,
with 700 white men and 1200 Indians was encamped at Dolsen's farm, about 15 miles from
the mouth of the Thames, on its northern
bank, and 56 miles from Detroit by water.
This news roused the Americans to still greater

exertions, and when they halted for a night's rest they had marched 25 miles from Sandwich, their starting point.

"The pursuit was renewed the next morning at dawn, and near the mouth of the Thames Johnson captured a lieutenant and eleven privates, who had just begun to destroy a bridge over a small stream emptying into that river. That made it evident to the Americans that Proctor had heard they were in pursuit of him and they hastened on, hoping to overtake, fight, and defeat him. That night they encamped on Drake's farm, four miles below Dolsen's.

"As the troops moved on, Perry's vessels had passed up the river to cover their movements when they should cross the Thames or its tributaries; but here there was a change in the character of the banks; below the river flowed on between prairies, its channel broad, its current sluggish, but here the country became hilly, the stream narrow and rapid, the banks high and wooded, affording convenient places for Indian ambuscades, from whence shots could be fired down upon the passing vessels below. So it was thought better not to take them any higher up the stream than Dolsen's, and Perry landed and offered his serivces to Harrison as volunteer aid; so joining the army in the exciting pursuit of the foe.

"The cowardly Proctor—much to the disgust of Tecumseh—fled up the Thames 28½ miles from Dolson's to Chatham, where an impassable stream called M'Gregor's Creek empties into that river. On reaching the spot he said to Tecumseh, 'Here we will defeat Harrison or lay our bones.'

"Tecumseh was pleased with both the speech and the spot, and remarked that when he looked at these streams he would be reminded of the Tippecanoe and the Wabash.

"Two bridges—one at the mouth of the creek and the other at a mill a mile above, had been partially destroyed, and at each was a party of Indians ready to dispute the passage of the Americans should they attempt to cross or to make repairs; but Major Wood, with two six-pounder cannon, and Colonel Johnson with his horsemen, soon sent them flying after Proctor."

"Was anybody hurt in either fight, papa?" asked Grace.

"Yes; 2 men of Johnson's party were killed, and 6 or 7 wounded. The Indians had a large number wounded and 13 killed. It was here that the chief Walk-in-the-Water with 60 warriors came to Harrison and offered to join his army conditionally. But Harrison had no time to attend to him, so told him if he left

Tecumseh, he must keep out of the way of the
American army."

"Did he do it, papa?" asked Elsie.

"Yes, he went back to the Detroit River."

"And did the Americans go on chasing the
British, papa?"

"Yes, and the British retreating, destroying
all they could on the way, firing houses and
vessels containing military and naval stores as
they went, the Americans following, putting
out the fires and saving houses, vessels, stores
as far as possible.

"But they did not catch up to the British
that night; they encamped and Harrison set a
double guard; which was well, for at midnight
Proctor and Tecumseh reconnoitred the camp,
but did not venture to attack it.

"At dawn the Americans were again in
motion, the mounted regiments in front, led by
General Harrison and his staff, the Kentucky
volunteers under General Shelby following.
It was not long before they had captured two
of the enemy's gunboats and several bateaux
with army supplies and ammunition, and some
prisoners.

"It was only nine o'clock when they reached
a place where the river was fordable by horses.
Harrison decided to cross there and each of the
mounted men took an infantryman on his horse

behind him; others crossed in the bateaux, and by noon the whole American army was on the north side of the river."

"I should think they must have been tired," said little Elsie. "Didn't they stop to rest a while, papa?"

"No, indeed," replied her father, stroking her hair and smiling down into the interested little face upturned to his, "they were much too eager to catch and defeat their country's foes. They hastened on as rapidly as possible, passing on their way many evidences of the rapidity of Proctor's retreat.

"It was two o'clock and they were eight miles from the crossing place when they came upon smouldering embers that showed where the enemy's rear guard had been but a short time before. By that they knew they were not far behind the foe, and Colonel Johnson dashed forward to learn their exact whereabouts.

"It was not long before he had captured a British wagoner who told him that Proctor had halted only three hundred yards farther on. Johnson, with Major James Suggett and his spies, moved cautiously on, and found the British drawn up in battle order, waiting for the coming of the Americans.

"He, Johnson, learned enough about their position to enable General Harrison and a coun-

cil of officers, held on horseback, to decide upon
the best order for the attack. The American
army now consisted of a little more than 3000
men—120 regulars of the 27th Regiment, 5
brigades of Kentucky volunteers under Governor Shelby, and Colonel Johnson's regiment of
mounted infantry.

"The foe had made choice of a good place
to make a stand. On one side was the Thames
River, with high and precipitous bank, on the
other a marsh running almost parallel with the
river. Between the two, about three hundred
yards from the river, was a narrow swamp with
a strip of solid ground between it and the large
marsh. Almost the whole space between the
river and the marsh was covered with forest
trees—oaks, beeches, and sugar maples, with
very little undergrowth.

"The British regulars were formed in two lines
between the river and the small swamp; their
artillery planted in the road near the bank of the
stream. The Indians were posted between the
two swamps, those commanded by Tecumseh
in person on the isthmus or narrowest point.

"At first Harrison arranged for the horsemen
to fall back and let the infantry make the first
attack, which would begin the battle; next the
cavalry were to charge the British. But when
all the preparations were completed Major

Wood, who had been reconnoitring the enemy's position, informed Harrison that the British were drawn up in open order, and, though contrary to all precedent, the general immediately decided to change his plan of attack. Instead of having the infantry fall upon the British front he ordered Johnson to charge their line with his mounted troops.

"In explaining his motive for the change, in a report rendered afterward to the Secretary of War, he said: 'The American backwoods men ride better in the woods than any other people. A musket or rifle is no impediment, they being accustomed to carrying them on horseback from their earliest youth. I was persuaded, too, that the enemy would be quite unprepared for the shock, and that they could not resist it.'

"The event speedily proved the wisdom of the decision. The general's orders were promptly obeyed, then a bugle sounded, and the Americans moved coolly forward, neither hesitating nor with undue haste, among huge trees, over fallen timber, and through the undergrowth, those impediments in their path compelling them to move slowly.

"While they were still at some distance from the front line of the British regulars the latter opened upon them with a severe fire, which caused some confusion at the head of the column, the horses of some of them taking fright; and before order was restored there came second volley. Then with a tremendous shout the American cavalry boldly dashed upon the British line and broke it, scattering it in all directions. Then the second line, thirty paces in the rear, was treated in the same way, and the horsemen wheeled right and left, pouring a destructive fire upon the rear of the confused and broken columns, so increasing their panic that they threw down their arms and surrendered as fast as they could.

"Lossing tells us that in less than five minutes after the first shot was fired the whole British force, more than eight hundred strong, were totally vanquished, and most of them made prisoners; only about fifty men and a single officer escaping."

"Ah, that was a victory to be proud of!" cried Lulu. "And what became of the brave Proctor, papa?"

"He fled from the field as fast as his horses would carry him, taking with him his personal staff, a few dragoons, and some mounted Indians. In the words of the old song

" ' When Proctor saw lost was the day,
He fled La Tranche's plain :
A carriage bore the chief away,
Who ne'er returned again.'

He was hotly pursued by a part of Johnson's corps under Major Payne."

"I think I remember, though, that they did not succeed in catching him," remarked Rosie.

"No," said the captain; "ten of them continued the pursuit until dark, but could not overtake him."

"Ah, it seems he was better at running away than at fighting," said Walter; "but if I remember right, he had to abandon his fine carriage."

"He did so; left the road and escaped by some bypath," replied Captain Raymond. "So rapid and masterly was his retreat that within twenty-four hours he was sixty-five miles distant from his starting point—the battle ground."

"And the American officers and men got nothing for their long chase, papa?" Grace said enquiringly.

"A trifle more," returned the captain, with a slightly amused look: "Major Wood captured Proctor's carriage, sword, and valuable papers. There were some beautifully written letters from Proctor's wife, in which she addresses him as 'Dear Henry.'"

"'Dear Henry,' indeed!" cried Lucilla scornfully. "I could never love such a coward. Nor—nor such a cruel wretch—delighting in

seeing men, women, and children tortured by
the savages, if he didn't take part in it with
his own hands. But you haven't finished the
story of the battle, papa."

"No, not quite. General Henry, with his
advancing columns, was hardly in sight of the
combatants before that part of the battle was
over; but at the same time that one bugle
sounded for that attack another was heard on
the left. Colonel Johnson and his troops moved
against the Indians almost at the same instant
that the first battalion—under his brother
James and Major Payne—attacked the British
regulars. He had divided his force and led
them—the second battalion—across the little
swamp to attack the Indian left. They were
in front of Shelby, with a company of infantry.
Harrison had taken a position on the extreme
right, near the bank of the river, where he
could observe and direct all the movements,
and with him were Adjutant-General Butler,
Commodore Perry, and General Cass.

"Tecumseh's savages reserved their fire till
the Americans were within a few paces of
them, then hurled upon them a deadly shower
of bullets, wounding General Johnson very
severely, and prostrating more than half his
vanguard of forlorn hope. On this part of the
field the undergrowth and the branches of the

trees were too thick to allow mounted men to do much service with their rifles, therefore Johnson ordered them to dismount and fight on foot at close quarters. They obeyed, and there were many hand to hand fights, the Kentuckians as they fought raising now and again the fearful cry, 'Remember the River Raisin.'"

"What did they mean by that, papa?" asked Elsie.

"I will explain that at another time," he replied. "You may ask for the story tomorrow. And now, to go on with this—for a while it seemed doubtful which side would win; but General Shelby, perceiving it, ordered the regiment of Lieutenant-Colonel Donaldson to the support of Johnson, and General King to press forward to the front with his brigade.

"The Indians had already recoiled from the shock of the Kentucky riflemen, and now they fled; they were pursued and a scattering running fight ended the battle. Proctor was running away as fast as he could, like some hunted wild animal, and his savage allies scattered themselves through the forest behind the larger swamp."

"Tecumseh with the rest, papa?" asked Elsie.

"No, my child, Tecumseh was lying dead on the field of battle. But for his loss it is likely the Indians would have continued the struggle for some time longer."

"Who killed him, papa?" she asked.

"No one can say certainly," replied her father, "though probably it was Johnson. Tradition and history tell us that Tecumseh had wounded Colonel Johnson with a rifle bullet, and was springing forward to tomahawk him, when Johnson drew a pistol from his belt and shot him through the heart. It is said that Johnson himself never either affirmed or denied that his was the hand which slew Tecumseh. Probably he did not really know whether the Indian he had killed was the great chieftain or some other. However, it is certain that he, Tecumseh, was slain in that battle,—as it seems he had predicted that he would be,—and it is a question of little importance whose hand sped the bullet or struck the blow that ended his career."

There was a moment of silence, broken by Grandma Elsie's soft voice:

> " ' The moment was fearful: a mightier foe
>   Had ne'er swung his battle axe o'er him;
> But hope nerved his arm for a desperate blow
>   And Tecumseh fell prostrate before him.
> He fought in defence of his kindred and king
>   With spirit most loving and loyal,
> And long shall the Indian warrior sing
>   The deeds of Tecumseh the royal.'

I presume you are right, captain, in thinking," she added, "that even Johnson himself did not know whether the Indian he had shot was Tecumseh, but as you have just said, the question is of no historical importance. We do know, however, that Johnson behaved most gallantly in the battle of the Thames and was sorely wounded in the hip, thigh, and hand; the last from the Indian whom he shot. He was disabled and said to his friend, Dr. Theobald, one of his staff, fighting near him, 'I am severely wounded: where shall I go?' Theobald, saying, 'Follow me,' led him across the smaller swamp to the road and the stand of Governor Shelby's surgeon-general. Johnson was faint from the loss of blood, and his horse, it would seem, was still more sorely wounded, for as his master was lifted from his back he fell dead."

"Oh, did the man die too, grandma?" asked little Elsie, with a look of eager interest and concern.

"No, dear; they gave him water, dressed his wounds, and carried him on board a vessel they had taken from the British. Captain Champlin, the commander of the *Scorpion*, was there on it; he took the colonel down the river in that vessel to his own, lying at Dolsen's, and from there, in her, to Detroit."

"Papa, did he get well and go back and fight some more?" asked Ned.

"No, my son; he went into Congress and served his country well there. But now it is high time for you and Elsie to go to your berths. Bid us all good-night; to-morrow you may ask as many questions as you please, and papa will answer them to the best of his ability."

CHAPTER VIII.

THE wind had risen while Captain Raymond
was talking, and now began to blow briskly,
bringing with it an occasional dash of rain; a
state of affairs that presently sent the whole
party into the cabin, and a little later they had
all retired to their staterooms but the captain
and his two older daughters, who lingered
a few moments for the bit of chat with their
dearly loved father of which they were so fond.

"Do you think we are going to have a hard
storm, papa?" Grace asked a little anxiously,
as she came to him to say good-night.

"I hope not," he said, "do not be anxious;
remember, 'the Lord hath his way in the whirl-
wind and in the storm, and the clouds are the
dust of his feet. He rebuketh the sea and
maketh it dry.' Remember, too, that 'the
Lord is good, a stronghold in the day of trouble;
and He knoweth them that trust in Him.'"

"Oh, yes! Thank you for reminding me of
those sweet words, father, dear," she returned
with a sigh of relief, and laying her cheek
affectionately against his as he put an arm about

132

her and held her close for a moment. "I will trust and not be afraid."

"That is right, daughter," he said; "no real evil can befall us while trusting in Him."

"But, papa, Christians do have great and real distresses sometimes," she returned, with an enquiring and slightly troubled look up into his face.

"Yes, daughter, 'Whom the Lord loveth he chasteneth and scourgeth every son whom he receiveth.' But 'like as a father pitieth his children so the Lord pitieth them that fear Him;' and He will sustain them under all the troubles that He sends. Remember that His promise is, 'As thy days, so shall thy strength be.'"

"Such a sweet, precious promise, papa!" she said. "I will just put my dear ones and myself in His care, trust in Him, and not lie awake, dreading shipwreck."

"That is what I would have you do, my darling," he returned. Do not forget those sweet words of Holy Writ: 'The Lord knoweth them that trust in Him,' nor the promise that He will never leave or forsake them. Put yourself into His care and go to sleep untroubled by doubts and fears. Good-night," he concluded, as he kissed her tenderly and let her go.

"And how is it with my dear eldest

daughter?" he asked, turning to Lucilla, who stood near awaiting her turn.

"I am not naturally so timid as Gracie, you know, papa," she answered, smiling up into his face as he passed an arm about her and drew her close to his side, while with the other hand he smoothed her hair caressingly, "and I do believe that God will take care of us all through the instrumentality of my own dear father, who knows so well how to manage a vessel in calm or storm. But you do not think there is much if any danger, do you, papa?" she asked, gazing searchingly into his face, "for you are not looking at all anxious."

"There is a pretty stiff breeze," he said, "and Erie is a stormy lake, owing to the shallowness of its waters, and the consequent liability to a heavy ground swell which renders its navigation particularly difficult and dangerous; but I have passed over it a number of times and do not feel any great amount of anxiety in regard to our safety—if I attend properly to my duty as commander of the *Dolphin*," he concluded, with his pleasant smile. "I must return to the deck, now; so good-night, daughter dear. May you sleep sweetly and peacefully, trusting in the care of your earthly father, and still more in that of your heavenly one."

"Oh, just one minute more, papa," she said entreatingly, as he released her. "I—I want to say that I am afraid that I was—almost, if not quite, a little disrespectful to you once or twice to-day."

"Ah! Well, darling, if you have been, it is entirely forgiven; so go to your bed in peace. I must hurry on deck and cannot wait to talk with you further now."

With the concluding words he hastened away, while she looked after him with eyes full of filial love, then as he disappeared she made her way as quickly as the rolling of the vessel would allow, across the saloon and joined her sister in their stateroom.

There were tears in Grace's sweet blue eyes as she lifted them to her sister's face.

"What, crying, Gracie darling?" Lulu asked, with concern.

"Yes; to think of poor papa out on deck in the wind and rain, while we are so comfortable in here," answered Grace with a sob, pulling out her handkerchief to wipe her eyes. "Oh, I almost wish I were a big, strong sailor, and knew all about managing a vessel, so that I could take his place and have him to his berth to rest and sleep."

"I'm sure I wish I could," sighed Lulu. "He should never have an ache or pain of any kind

if I might bear them for him; never be anything but the happiest man in the world if——"
but she paused suddenly, while a vivid blush
suffused her face. "I have no right to talk so,"
she added in a remorseful tone, "I, who so
often fail to be the perfectly respectful and
cheerfully obedient daughter that I ought."

"I really think you judge yourself very
hardly, Lu," remarked Grace, with a surprised
glance into her sister's face. "You are always
perfectly obedient and very affectionate toward
our dear father, seeming to take great delight
in doing everything you can to please him and
add to his comfort; I really do not think he has a
child who loves him better or does more for his
comfort; no, not even I, who esteem him the
very best and dearest father in the world," she
concluded, with a look and smile that said more
than her words.

"Oh, thank you, Gracie! I do love him
dearly, dearly; but as you know I am shame-
fully quick-tempered and wilful and sometimes
look vexed at a reproof or prohibition, then the
next minute could beat myself well for it."

"Lu, you never, never are in a passion nowadays!" exclaimed Grace. "I own you do
look vexed sometimes for a minute or two, but
then it's all over and you are just as sweet and
pleasant as anyone could wish. Oh, you are

just the dearest, dearest girl! Ah, you needn't shake your head and look so dolorous," she added, in a playful tone, putting her arms about Lucilla and kissing her with ardent affection.

"Ah, yes, you are all so dear and loving, so ready to excuse my faults," Lulu said, returning the embrace with interest. "No one more so than our dear father, though I well know I have given him more pain and trouble than any other of his children, if not than all put together. Gracie, let us kneel down together and ask God to take care of papa and all of us, and that if it is His will the storm may soon so abate that our dear father can go to his berth and get a good night's rest."

Grace was more than willing, and they spent some minutes in earnest supplication.

In that act of prayer Grace cast all her care upon the Lord, and scarcely had she more than laid her head upon her pillow before she fell asleep; but Lucilla lay for hours listening to the howling of the wind, the sound of the waves dashing against the sides of the vessel, her father's voice occasionally giving an order through the speaking trumpet, and the hurried and heavy tread of the sailors as they hastened to obey. It seemed a worse storm than any she had ever been in upon the water, and almost her every breath was a prayer for the safety of the yacht with all its living freight—especially her dearly loved father, now exposed to the fury of the wind, waves, and rain—that they might pass through it in safety.

But at last she fell into a deep sleep, and for some hours heard and felt nothing of the storm. Yet it was not over when she awoke; she could still hear the howling of the wind, the rush of the waters, and feel the rolling and pitching of the vessel. But it was daylight, and slipping from her berth with care not to rouse her still sleeping sister, she knelt for a moment of heart-felt thanks to her heavenly Father, that thus far they had weathered the storm, and fervent supplication that the vessel might outride it in safety to the end.

Rising from her knees she made a hasty toilet, then, anxious to learn of her father's welfare, stole from the room, and holding on by the furniture, crossed the saloon, then with some difficulty climbed the cabin stairway and reached the windswept deck.

One glance showed her her father standing at a little distance, giving some direction to a sailor. He did not see her. There was a momentary lull in the wind, and taking advantage of it she started on a run toward him. But just at that moment came another and fierce gust that took her off her feet and swept her toward the side of the vessel.

In another instant she would have been in the water, had her father not turned suddenly and caught her in his arms barely in time to save her from that fate. He held her fast with one arm while he grasped the railing with the other hand, and held on till the gale again moderated for a moment. Then he carried her back to the cabin. They were alone there, for the others were still in their staterooms. He strained her to his breast in silence, and she felt a tear fall on her head.

"Thank God, my darling, precious child is safe in my arms!" he said at last, speaking scarcely above a whisper, pressing his lips again and again to her forehead, her cheek, her mouth.

"And my own dear father saved me," she said in quivering tones, her arms about his neck, her face half hidden on his breast.

"It was a narrow escape, my child," he sighed, repeating his caresses, "a very narrow escape; and what would I have done had I lost my dear eldest daughter? You must not try it again; don't venture on deck again until I give you permission."

"I will not, papa," she returned. "But oh, haven't you been up all night? can't you take some rest now?"

"Not yet; perhaps after a little. There, there, do not look so distressed," smoothing her hair caressingly as he spoke. "You must remember I am an old sailor and used to such vigils. I had a cup of coffee and a biscuit a while ago which quite refreshed me."

"But can't you go to your berth now and take some hours of rest and sleep, papa, dear?" she asked entreatingly, her eyes gazing lovingly into his. "Surely someone among your men must be fit to take charge of the yacht for a while."

"Not just yet, daughter; perhaps before long I can do so. I must leave you now and go back to my duties; and do you go to your state-room and thank your heavenly Father for your escape from a watery grave."

With that he released her and hurried away up the cabin stairs, she following him with looks of yearning affection till he disappeared from view, then hastening to obey his parting injunction.

Her heart was full of love and gratitude to God for her spared life, and that thus far they had escaped shipwreck, and even as she gave thanks it seemed to her that there was a lull in the storm—the wind almost ceasing to blow and the vessel rocking much less.

"Oh, Gracie," she said, as she rose from her

knees and perceived that her sister's eyes were open, "I do think—I do hope that the worst of the storm is over."

"Do you?" cried Grace joyously, hastily throwing back the covering and stepping out upon the floor. "Oh, how glad I am! How good God has been to us all! But where is papa? Has he been up all night?"

"Yes," replied Lulu, "and oh, Gracie, if it hadn't been for him I would be at the bottom of the lake now," she added, with tears of gratitude filling her eyes.

"Why, Lu!" exclaimed Grace in astonishment, "you surely did not venture up on the deck in this storm?"

"I did, and was nearly blown into the lake, but papa caught me, held me fast for a minute, then carried me down into the cabin."

"Oh, Lu! Lu! I hope you will never venture so again! I'd be broken-hearted, and so would papa, and indeed, all the rest, if we lost you in that way. What could I ever do without my dear, big sister?" she concluded, putting her arms about Lucilla and holding her fast in a most loving embrace.

"Oh, but it is nice that you love me so, Gracie, dear," Lulu returned.

"It was very foolish in me to venture on deck in such a gale, but papa did not scold me at all; just held me fast, petting and caressing me as if I were one of his greatest treasures."

"Of course," said Grace. "But didn't he forbid you to try going on deck again before the wind dies down?"

"Yes," acknowledged Lulu. "Oh, I wish he could stay below too. I want him to go to his berth and sleep off his fatigue. He must be very tired after his long night's vigil. But it is nearly breakfast time, and we should be making ourselves neat to appear at the table, looking as papa would have us."

An hour later all had gathered about the table, the captain at the head of it as usual, and looking cheerful and pleasant-tempered as was his wont, though somewhat weary and worn. He reported the storm nearly over, no serious damage done the vessel, nor much time lost. He hoped to be in the Welland Canal before night, and that they would find themselves on Lake Ontario when they woke in the morning.

"And can you not go to your berth for some hours' rest and sleep when you have finished your breakfast, my dear?" queried Violet, with a loving, anxious look into his face.

"Probably; after a short visit to the deck to see that all is going right there. Excuse me, my dear," he added, pushing away his plate and rising to his feet as he spoke. "I must return to my duties at once, but would have everyone else finish the meal at leisure," and with the last word he hurried away.

"My dear papa looks so tired, mamma," remarked little Elsie in regretful tones, "what has he been doing?"

"Staying up all night to take care of us," replied Violet, the tears shining in her eyes. "Don't you think we ought to love dear papa and do all we can to make him happy?"

"Yes, indeed, mamma!" answered the little girl earnestly. "Oh, I hope he can get a good sleep soon so that he will feel rested and well. I was going to ask him to tell me about what happened at the River Raisin. You know our soldiers, in that fight with the British and Indians that he told us about yesterday, called out over and over again, 'Remember the River Raisin,' and papa said he would tell me what it meant if I would ask him to-day. But I can wait till to-morrow," she added, with a sigh of resignation.

"How would it do for grandma to take your papa's place and tell you the story?" asked Grandma Elsie, in cheerful tones, and with a loving, smiling look at the little girl.

"Oh, nicely, grandma! I don't know but

you could do it as well as papa could," answered
the child eagerly.

"Ah, dearie, it is a very sad story, and I
think I shall have to make it short," sighed
Mrs. Travilla; "the details would but harrow
up your feelings unnecessarily."

"Bad doings of the British and Indians,
grandma?" queried the little girl.

"Yes; it was that, indeed!" said Mr. Dinsmore; "the latter part of the tragedy a terrible
slaughter of defenceless prisoners—tortured,
scalped, tomahawked, slain in various ways
with the utmost cruelty; many of them burned
alive in the houses where they lay wounded,
unable to move. It was a fearful slaughter
which Proctor, far from trying to prevent,
rewarded with praise and the purchase of the
scalps."

"Oh, wasn't he a very, very bad man, grandpa?" exclaimed little Elsie.

"More of a devil than a man, I should say,"
exclaimed Walter. "I remember reading an
extract from a letter written a few days later,
from Fort Malden, by a Kentuckian to his
mother, in which he says, 'Never, dear mother,
should I live a thousand years can I forget
the frightful sight of this morning, when
hideously painted Indians came into the fort,
some of them carrying half a dozen scalps of

my countrymen fastened upon sticks and yet covered with blood, and were congratulated by Colonel Proctor for their bravery."

"But all the British officers were not so cruel, Walter, my dear," said his mother. "I remember the story of the letter to which you refer, and that the writer went on to say that he heard two British officers talking of that scene together; that one of them, whose name, he had been told, was Lieutenant-Colonel St. George, remarked to the other that Proctor was a disgrace to the British army, that such encouragement to devils was a blot upon the British character."

"Oh, please, grandma," cried little Elsie in distress, "I don't want to hear any more of that story."

"No, dear, it is far from being a pleasant one, nor is it worth while to harrow up your feelings with it," returned Mrs. Travilla. "I will try to find some pleasanter one for you and Neddie boy to help you pass the time agreeably while the storm prevents us from enjoying ourselves upon the deck."

With that all rose and left the table to gather in the saloon for morning worship, which, in the captain's absence, was conducted by Mr. Dinsmore.

But the storm was abating so that in another

half hour Captain Raymond felt it safe to leave the deck and retire to his stateroom for much needed rest and sleep, and the others could sit comfortably in the saloon, the ladies with their fancy work, while Grandma Elsie entertained the little folks with stories suited to their tender years.

Walter, too, was one of the listeners for a time, then with his grandfather ventured upon deck to take an observation of the weather and their surroundings. When they returned it was with the cheering report that the storm had evidently spent its fury, the wind had nearly died down, the rain ceased to fall, and the sun was struggling through the clouds.

"Oh, then we can go up on deck, can't we, grandpa?" cried Neddie, in eager tones.

"After a little, sonny," returned his grandpa, sitting down and drawing the young pleader to his knee.

"When my papa wakes up?" queried Neddie, in a slightly disappointed tone.

"Yes, indeed, Ned," said Lucilla, "for though I am so much older than you, papa forbade me to go up there without his permission."

"Why did he, Lu?" asked Elsie in a tone of surprise; "and haven't you been up there at all this morning?"

"Yes, I was, before papa had forbidden me

—and would have been blown into the lake if he hadn't caught me in his arms and held me fast."

"Oh, Lu, tell us all about it!" cried Ned, while the others who had not heard the story expressed their surprise in various ways and asked question upon question.

"There's hardly anything more to tell," replied Lucilla. "I know papa is always on deck early in the morning, and as I wake early too, I have a habit of running up there to exchange morning greetings with him. That was what I went for this time, not at all realizing how hard the wind was blowing, but I had scarcely set foot on the deck when it took my skirts and sent me across toward the spot where papa stood holding on to the railing with one hand, his speaking trumpet in the other. He dropped that in an instant and threw his arm round me." As she spoke she shuddered at the thought of her narrow escape from a watery grave, and her voice trembled with emotion. Controlling it with an effort, "You see," she concluded, "that I owe my life to my dear father, and—and I love him even better than ever, though I thought before that I loved him as much as was possible."

At that Violet dropped her work, went quickly to Lucilla's side, and bending down over her, kissed her with warmth of affection.

"Oh, I am so glad—so thankful that he was able to do it," she said in trembling tones and with tears in her eyes. "Dear Lu, it would have broken our hearts to lose you in that sudden, dreadful way."

"As it would mine to lose you, dear Mamma Vi," returned Lucilla with emotion, putting her arms about Violet's neck and returning her caresses with interest, "for you are so very good, kind, and loving that I have grown very fond of you. And I know it would break papa's heart to lose you, even more than to lose me or all of his children."

"Oh, I hope he may never be so tried! for I know he loves us all very dearly, as we do him," said Violet. "I don't know what any of us could do without him."

CHAPTER IX.

The sun was just peeping above the horizon, the yacht moving swiftly and steadily onward as Lucilla stepped from the companion-way upon the deck, the next morning, having obtained permission the night before to do so in case the quiet movements of the vessel made it certain she would run no such risk as she had the previous day.

Her father was pacing the deck, and so near that he took her hand the moment she appeared.

"My early bird, as usual! Good-morning, daughter mine," he said in tender tones as he bent down and bestowed upon her the caress she never failed to receive from him when first they met at the beginning of a new day.

"Good-morning, dear, dear papa, yesterday's saver of my life," she returned, in moved tones, putting her arms about his neck and pressing her lips to his again and again. "Oh, father, surely I belong to you more than ever now!"

"You are my very own, one of my chief treasures," he said, in response to that. "God

149

bless my darling and have her ever in His kind care and keeping!" He clasped her hand tenderly in his as he spoke, and for a while they paced the deck together.

"Oh, where are we, papa?" she asked, gazing from side to side in eager curiosity. "This wide expanse of water cannot be the Welland Canal?"

"No, we passed through that in the night, and are now in Lake Ontario."

"Oh, I am glad we are so far on our journey," she said, "and the water is so quiet that it seems a very suitable place in which to spend this sweet Sabbath day."

"I think so, if only we try to spend it aright."

"I do intend to," she responded. "And we shall have our usual service in the morning; we younger ones a Bible lesson with papa in the afternoon, won't we?"

"I think so," he said. "I certainly expect to give my own children a Bible lesson, and we will not shut out any who may choose to take a part in it. That would be very selfish, would it not?"

"Yes, sir! yes, indeed! I think so, for you always make a Bible lesson very interesting as well as instructive."

"I am glad my daughter finds it so," he said, smiling down upon her.

They moved silently back and forth for a few minutes, Lucilla apparently in deep thought, her father watching with keen and loving interest the changeful expression of her features.

"What is it, daughter? Of what are you thinking?" he asked at length.

"About the narrow escape of yesterday, papa," she answered, lifting to his a face full of solemn awe. "I was asking myself, as I have many times since my narrow escape of yesterday morning, Was I ready for heaven? Would I have gone there if I had been drowned without time to think and prepare to meet my Judge? Oh, father, can anyone be saved without time to think and repent of every wrong thought and feeling, and asking God's forgiveness for it? And how would it be possible to do all that while struggling for your life?"

"Daughter," he said in tender tones, "are you not forgetting these sweet words of Holy Writ: 'He that believeth on the Son hath everlasting life?' Take notice, it is not shall have, but *hath*. It is not only the sins already committed which God forgives for Jesus' sake when He adopts us for His own, but those also which in His omniscience He sees that we will be guilty of before the work of sanctification is finished. If we are truly His, they are all forgiven in advance. He says: 'I give unto them eternal life; and they shall never perish, neither shall any man pluck them out of my hand. My Father which gave them me is greater than all; and no man is able to pluck them out of my Father's hand. I and my Father are one.' In another place he says, 'Verily, verily, I say unto you, He that heareth my word and believeth on Him that sent me *hath* everlasting life and shall not come into condemnation; but *is passed from death unto life.*' The one important question is, are we really His? Have we accepted His offered salvation and given ourselves entirely to Him? If that be so we have no cause for anxiety or fear; for the Lord knoweth them that are His, and will never suffer any real evil to befall them. Death will be but going home to Him, and that with all the sin taken away and we made perfect in holiness, no want of conformity to His holy will left in us."

"Yes, papa, but——"

"But what, daughter?"

"Oh, if I should be mistaken in thinking that I really belong to Him! Papa, how can I know it?"

"Have you any doubt that you are mine?"

"No, indeed, papa, not the slightest."

"But how do you know it?"

"Because you have told me so again and

again; and besides, I have only to look in the glass to see that I have your features, that I resemble you about as much in looks as a young girl can resemble a——"

"Middle-aged man," he added, finishing the sentence for her as she paused with an earnest, loving look up into his face.

"And the Bible tells us," he continued, "that 'Whom He did foreknow He also did predestinate to be conformed to the image of His Son.' If we are really His, we will, in a greater or less degree, resemble Him and will be changed into the same image from glory to glory."

"Do you see anything of His image in me, papa?" she asked anxiously, humbly.

"I am glad, very glad to be able to say that I think I do, daughter," he replied joyously, tenderly. "For years past I have watched you very closely, constantly praying God to bless my efforts to train you up in the way you should go, and bring you to Him, and I am very happy to say that for a long while now I have seen that you were striving earnestly to overcome your faults and live as a true disciple of Christ. And had you been snatched from me in that sudden way, while the loss of my dear child would have been terrible to me, I should not have mourned as those without hope;

but should now be looking forward to a happy meeting with you in that blessed land where sin and sorrow and death are unknown."

"Thank you, dear papa, oh, thank you very much!" she said, with emotion. "If I am a Christian it is because you have taken almost infinite pains to make me such, to point me to Christ and lead the way; the way that you made plainer to me than anyone else ever did."

"Give all the glory and praise to God, my darling," he responded, in moved tones. "It has been my daily, earnest prayer, that He would give me wisdom for the work of bringing my children to Him and bless my efforts, and I think my petition has been granted. When you see a work laid to your hands for which you feel incompetent, ask help from on high, remembering and pleading His gracious promise—'If any of you lack wisdom let him ask of God, that giveth to all men liberally and upbraideth not; and it shall be given him. But let him ask in faith, nothing wavering.' Never forget that last clause. God knows the heart, and it will be useless for us to plead with Him a promise which we do not really believe."

"Yes, papa; surely that would be insulting to even a human creature. Oh, pray for me, that I may have strong faith and never, never doubt one word of God's promises, or threats either, and that I may be always ready for whatever He sends. Oh, I can never thank Him enough for giving me such a good, kind, praying, Christian father!"

"And I have great reason for gratitude for the dear children he has bestowed upon me," her father responded, pressing the hand he held, "and for the hope that we will spend a blessed eternity together in that land where sin and sorrow are unknown."

"Yes, papa, what a delightful thought that is! and yet I cannot help feeling glad to stay a little longer here in this world. Oh, this is such a lovely morning and the view is as new to me as it is enchanting, for, as you know, in going to Chicago we passed over this part of the route in the night, so that I saw nothing of the scenery."

"Well, I think you may enjoy it to the full to-day," he returned, "and that some time in the afternoon you will get a sight of the Thousand Islands; though, by the way, counting all, big and little, there are fifteen hundred or more."

"Then we won't stop at all of them?"

"Hardly," he answered with a smile. "They fill the river for twenty-seven miles along its course. Most of them are mere rocky islets,

covered generally with stunted hemlocks and
cedar trees down to the water's edge. Some
are square miles in extent and others only a few
yards."

"And how wide is the river where they are,
papa?"

"It varies from two to nine miles in width.
Canoes and small boats may pass safely among
all the islands, and there is a deep channel for
steamboats and large vessels which, having a
rocky bottom, never varies in depth or position."

"Do they belong to our country or to Canada, papa? I ought to know, but, if I ever
did, I have forgotten."

"The boundary line, which was determined
in 1818, passes among them. Grindstone,
Carleton, and Wells are the names of the
largest of those belonging to the United States,
and Grand and Howe of those belonging to
Canada."

"And there are a good many stories connected with them, are there not, papa?"

"Yes; perhaps one of these days we will
hunt them up; for I know that my children—
to say nothing of older people—are fond of
stories."

"Especially when told by our father, who is
sure to make them interesting," she said, with

an upward glance into his face that spoke volumes of love and admiration.

"Ah, such, it seems, is the opinion of my partial eldest daughter, who can see nothing in her father but what is good and admirable."

"A weakness equally shared by his wife," remarked a clear, sweet voice in their rear.

They turned quickly at the sound, the captain exclaiming, as he let go his daughter's hand, put an arm about Violet, bent down and kissed her tenderly, "This is a most agreeable surprise, my dearest, for I left you, at least, so I thought, fast asleep. I moved as quietly as I could, not wishing to disturb your slumbers."

"As you always do move on such occasions, my best and dearest of husbands," she responded, returning his caresses. "You made no noise, but somehow I happened to wake just as you closed the door, and thinking I would secure for myself the rare treat of an early walk with my—better half, I left my berth promptly and began my toilet. So here I am, to spoil Lu's private morning interview with the almost idolized father she considers her peculiar property at this hour of the day."

"Ah!" he returned laughingly, "I put it the other way. She is my property, yet hardly more so than my lovely young wife."

"Yes; you and I belong to each other, and Lu can say the same to you," laughed Violet. "Can't you, Lu?"

"So I think, Mamma Vi," returned Lucilla, "and though probably you are nearer and dearer to him than I, you cannot say as I can, that you have his blood in your veins and have belonged to him ever since you were born."

"No," acknowledged Violet, "but I can say I belong to him of choice, you only of necessity."

"Oh, that doesn't matter!" laughed Lucilla; "since if I had the privilege of choosing, I should be all the same his very, very own. That is, if he would have me," she added, with a look of ardent affection up into her father's face, and laying her hand upon his shoulder.

"There is no question about that, dear child," he said, putting his arm round her waist again. "Since the day I first heard of your birth there has not been one in which I have not thanked God for this good gift of His to me," he concluded, with a fond caress.

"So you see you have no need to be jealous even of me, Lu," Violet said, with pleased look and smile.

"No, I am not, Mamma Vi, not in the least; for I would far rather be papa's daughter than his wife. But, I suppose, you would rather have him to yourself for a while now, so I will go down——"

"No, no, Lu dear, stay here with us," interrupted Violet, while the captain drew his daughter a little closer, saying, "Stay where you are. Cannot I have and enjoy you both at once?"

"Oh, I'm glad enough to be allowed to stay, if you both want me," exclaimed Lucilla, with a pleased little laugh. "But I thought I had had my turn and was afraid I'd be in the way now."

"When I find you in the way I shall not hesitate to give you an order to go below," her father said, with a look of amusement.

Then, taking her hand in his and giving the other arm to Violet, he resumed the interrupted promenade of the deck till they were joined by the children and older members of the family party.

Then came the summons to the breakfast table. All were in excellent spirits, greatly enjoying the pleasant change from yesterday's storm to the lovely weather of to-day. Most of the day was spent upon the deck holding the Sabbath services usual with them there, then in reading and conversation suited to the sacred time, or in gazing out over the waters, watching the passing vessels, and as they steamed from the lake into the St. Lawrence River and pursued their way among the islands there, gazing upon them with interest and curiosity.

"Are we going to stop at any of them, papa?" asked Grace.

"I think not," he replied. "We are in some haste to reach Montreal, as we hope to find letters there from the home folks."

"Yes," said Grandma Elsie, "I am hoping to hear from my boys—Harold and Herbert—that they have arrived safely at home; also for some news from all the other dear ones in that vicinity."

"And we hope it will be all good news," added Captain Raymond cheerily.

"And we will send despatches and letters to some of them, that all may be apprised of our safety thus far," added his wife.

"Yes, indeed," said Violet. "By the way, I wonder where our bride and groom are by this time? I wish we might come across them and persuade them to travel in the *Dolphin* again. We would only have to crowd a little as before, to make room for them."

"And none of us would object to that, I think," remarked Rose.

"I, for one, am decidedly of the opinion that

it would pay," said Lucilla. "Don't you think
so, father?"

"Yes; I have always found their society
enjoyable," Captain Raymond replied to that.
"And I hope they have found ours agreeable
enough to need but little urging to accept our
invitation."

"Perhaps we may come upon them in Montreal," remarked Grace. "Papa, is it not the
largest city of Lower Canada?"

"Yes; the largest in British America."

"Where is it, papa?" asked little Elsie.

"On the left bank of this—the St. Lawrence
River, 200 miles below Lake Ontario; 160
above Quebec, which will be our next stopping
place."

"Will we get there to-day, papa?" asked
Elsie.

"No," he replied. "To-day is nearly gone,
daughter. See, the sun is setting, and you and
Neddie will be going presently to your beds, to
have a good night's sleep, I hope, and be
ready to enjoy to-morrow's visit to Montreal."

CHAPTER X.

THE drip, drip of rain was the first sound that greeted Lucilla's ears on awaking the next morning. She started up in her berth and listened. The *Dolphin* was not moving.

"Oh, we must be anchored at Montreal, and it's raining," she said to herself. "There will not be much sight-seeing for us to-day, I'm afraid. Dear, dear! I hope we won't have to hurry away without seeing anything. Though in that case, perhaps papa will bring us here again next year."

She did not linger long over her toilet, and was soon with her father on the deck.

"Oh, papa!" she exclaimed, after the usual morning greetings had been exchanged, "aren't you sorry it has turned out a rainy day?"

"A bright one would seem pleasanter to us, as we had planned to do some sight-seeing," he replied, "but let us remember who sends the changes of the weather, that He knows what is best for us, and that we may safely trust in His knowledge, power, and love for us?"

"Yes, papa, that is how I ought to feel about

162

it, and I will try to," she said, a sweet smile replacing the sight frown that had marred the beauty of her face for the moment.

"I think," he went on presently, "that it is not going to be a lasting rain. Probably showery for some hours, which we can spend with advantage in a short review of the history of Montreal, and considering what parts of it are most worthy of our attention; for we cannot take time to visit every locality."

"Oh, what a nice idea, papa! It quite comforts me!" she cried, looking up into his face with a bright, glad smile, "I do think I have just the very best, kindest, wisest father——"

"There, there! that will do!" he said, stopping her flow of words with a kiss full upon her lips. "I am afraid my eldest daughter is a decided flatterer."

"Oh, papa, the truth isn't flattery, is it?" she asked with a roguish look up into his eyes.

"Ah! but silly young things, like my daughter Lucilla, oftentimes have vivid imaginations. But to change the subject, Montreal, you know, is historic ground."

"Yes, sir; I remember that the first white man who visited it was Jacques Quartier or Cartier, a French navigator. And didn't he discover the Gulf and River St. Lawrence? and give them those names?"

"Yes; and named the place here Mount Royal—in honor of his king, Francis I. The city is built upon an island thirty miles long and twelve wide, and upon the site of a noted Indian village called Hochelaga. Cartier's visit was paid in 1535. In 1640 a white settlement was gathered there. The Indians, friendly at first, afterward became jealous, then hostile. The whites at first defended their town with a stockade and slight bastions, but later with a strong wall of masonry fifteen feet high, with battlements and six gates."

"What an old, old town it is!" exclaimed Lucilla. "Did it become a large city very quickly, papa?"

"No; its growth was gradual, but when in the middle of the last century hostilities were begun between the French and English colonies, Montreal was an important frontier town. It was threatened by the English under Amherst in 1759, and in the autumn of the next year passed out of the possession of the French into that of the English."

"And they have kept it ever since?"

"Yes; though our people invaded it in 1775, after the capture of Forts St. John and Chambly."

"Oh, yes, sir! under Montgomery and Arnold, wasn't it?"

"The first attack was under Ethan Allen, and was made a month earlier than the taking of those forts," replied the captain. "Montgomery had sent him to arouse the people in favor of the rebellion, as our cause was then styled by our foes. Allen was active and brave, and soon had gathered 250 Canadians to his standard. He wrote, Lossing tells us, to Montgomery, that within three days he would join him, with at least 500 armed Canadians, in laying siege to St. John's.

"He was marching up the east side of the St. Lawrence when he fell in with Major Brown, at the head of an advanced party of Americans and Canadians, and Brown proposed that they should make a joint attack upon Montreal; telling Allen it was weak and defenceless. Allen agreed and they made their arrangements. Allen was to get canoes and cross the river below the city with his troops, while Brown was to cross above with 200 men, and they were to attack the city simultaneously.

"But for some unexplained reason Brown failed to keep his part of the agreement, and Allen's party made the attack alone.

"It was at night, a rough, windy night, that they, 80 Canadians and 30 Americans, crossed the river, and they had so few canoes that three crossings were necessary to carry the whole party over. That was safely accomplished by daylight, at which time Allen expected to hear Brown's signal, telling him that he too had crossed with his men. But the signal was waited for in vain. He did not come at all.

"Allen would have retreated if the boats could have carried all over at once; as it was, he placed guards on the roads to prevent people from carrying the news of his presence into the city. But in spite of that precaution the inhabitants somehow became aware of it, and soon troops were seen issuing from the gates. They consisted of a force of 40 British regulars, 200 Canadians, and a few Indians.

"Two to one of the Americans, if not more!" exclaimed Lucilla.

"Yes," said her father, "but so brave were our men that they fought for an hour and three-quarters before they would surrender. At last, however, they all deserted but 28, 7 of whom were wounded, and Allen agreed to surrender upon being promised honorable terms."

"The prisoners were marched to Montreal and well treated until General Prescott got them in his custody, when he behaved toward them in the most brutal manner. Learning that Allen was the man who captured Ticonderoga, he flew into a rage, threatened him with a halter, and ordered him to be bound hand and foot in irons and placed on board the war schooner *Gaspee.* A bar of iron eight feet long was attached to his fetters, his fellow-prisoners were fastened together in pairs with handcuffs, and all were thrust into the lowest part of the ship, where they were allowed neither bed nor seat."

"Oh, papa! what a monster of cruelty that Prescott must have been!" exclaimed Lucilla. "Was he not the same Prescott who had command of the British troops in Rhode Island some two years later?"

"The very same; a most unfit man for such a position as he held then and there. A cowardly wretch, a petty tyrant, with a callous heart, a narrow mind, and utterly destitute of benevolence or charity."

"But what became of Allen finally, papa? If I ever knew, I have forgotten."

"He was kept for five weeks in that deplorable condition, at Montreal, on board the *Gaspee;* then the vessel was sent down to Quebec, and he was put on board of another vessel, where he was treated humanely. He was sent to England to be tried for treason, and landed at Falmouth, where his grotesque garb attracted a great deal of attention. He was afterward sent to Halifax, Nova Scotia, and thence to New York, where, in May 1778, he was exchanged for Colonel Campbell."

"There is not nearly so much to be seen here as in Quebec, is there, papa?" she asked.

"No," he replied, "and we will not stay very long here, but will spend more of our time there."

"Oh, papa, didn't General Montgomery come to Montreal some time after the events you have been telling of?"

"Yes; after the fall of St. John's. Carleton knew the place was weak, and at once retreated on board of one of a number of small vessels lying in the river, as did General Prescott, several officers, and 120 private soldiers. But Montgomery, as soon as he was aware that they were trying to flee, sent Colonel Baston with continental troops, cannon, and armed gondolas to the mouth of the Sorel, where they were posted so advantageously that the British fleet could not pass, so were compelled to surrender. But Carleton escaped, in a boat with muffled oars, past the American post to Three Rivers, from which place he soon reached Quebec in safety."

"What a pity! I wish the Americans had been more watchful!" exclaimed Lucilla.

"They were watchful in their guard boats," replied her father, "but a dark night and secret way were in Carleton's favor. They secured Prescott, who certainly richly deserved to be made prisoner and treated far worse than he was, but that was by no means the loss to the British that the taking of Carleton would have been, for Prescott's conduct on many occasions made him a disgrace to their army. But we have had a long talk, and there is the call to breakfast."

In spite of the drip and splash of the rain outside the faces that surrounded the breakfast table were bright and cheery.

"There will be no going ashore to-day, I presume," remarked Grandma Elsie, when the blessing had been asked, and the filling of plates and coffee cups had begun.

"I do not despair of it, mother," returned the captain, in cheerful tones. "It does not seem to me like a settled rain. I think it will clear by noon, and that then we can go about the city and its environs in carriages."

"Yes," said Mr. Dinsmore, "though our own are beyond reach at present, it is altogether likely the city, in the persons of some of its inhabitants, supplies vehicles for those willing to pay for their use."

"No doubt of it," said the captain.

"Where is Walter, mamma?" queried Violet, noticing that the boy's seat was unoccupied.

"I do not know. I fear he has overslept himself," replied her mother.

"No, mother," said the captain; "he was early on deck and begged permission of me to go into the city in quest of our mail. Ah, here he comes," as a blithe boyish voice was heard at the head of the companion-way.

In another moment the lad entered, looking rosy and exultant.

"Mail for us all, not to speak of telegrams," he said, in lively tones, emptying his pockets as he spoke, and handing letters and papers to one and another. "Mamma, your share is a large one, as it ought to be; the telegram, from my brothers, I presume, to announce their safe arrival at home; it is the one at the top of the pile, as you may see," handing her a number of missives.

"Yes; and most satisfactory," she said, with a smile and a sigh of relief, as she opened and read it at a glance. "'Just arrived safely. Hear that all the relatives are well.' Ah, what cause for gratitude to the Giver of all good!" she exclaimed low and feelingly. "There have been so many accidents, yet we and our dear ones have escaped them all."

"It is indeed a cause for gratitude," responded her father. "We will trust in Him and not be afraid; for wherever we go we are under His kind care and protection."

"A most comforting and cheering thought," said the captain.

Grandma Elsie was opening a letter postmarked Newport, R. I.

"Ah, this is from our dear Molly!" she said. "She dates 'Paradise Valley.' Where is that?"

"It is on the island of Rhode Island, a few miles out from the City of Newport," replied the captain.

"Ah, yes; so she tells me," responded Mrs. Travilla, her eyes still upon the letter. "They have taken a furnished house for some months, there is another within a few yards of it, now empty, and they want us all to come there, help fill the two, and have a pleasant time for a few days, or weeks, enjoying the lovely scenery, the sea breeze, and each other's society. What do you all say to the proposition?"

"I think we might spend a short time as pleasantly there as anywhere else," said Mr. Dinsmore.

"As I do," said his wife.

"I only wish I could be of the party," sighed Walter, assuming a very depressed expression of countenance; "but my college duties will claim my attention before that."

"For which you may be very thankful, laddie," said his sister Rose. "Remember it is not every boy—or young man—who attains to the blessing of a college education, without having to earn it by hard work."

"I expect and intend to do hard work," returned Walter, stirring his coffee, for he had seated himself and was beginning a hearty breakfast.

"On which side is your vote to be cast, Violet, my dear?" asked the captain in his pleasant tones, turning inquiringly to his young wife.

"I think a brief visit there, on our homeward route, might be very enjoyable," she replied; "but if my husband prefers to go directly home I shall be entirely content."

"Thank you, my dear. I do not see any need of excessive haste in returning home, and it shall be just as you say, whether we accept Cousin Molly's invitation or decline it."

"Then suppose we leave it to Lu and Gracie to say what shall be done, so far as our immediate family is concerned."

"Very well," he said. "Speak freely, daughters, in regard to your preferences for accepting this invitation or going directly home after visiting Quebec."

"I shall be perfectly satisfied with my father's decision," said Lucilla, with a smiling look up into his face. "I have no doubt the little visit to Paradise Valley would prove very enjoyable, yet home is to me the sweetest place on earth, and we have been away from it a good many weeks already."

Captain Raymond looked not ill pleased with her reply, but turned inquiringly to Grace.

"I can echo my sister's sentiments, father dear," she said, with her own sweet smile; "keep me with you and I shall be content and happy wherever that may be."

The captain's answering smile seemed to say he thought no other man had daughters quite equal to his, but turning to Evelyn he asked what were her wishes in regard to the matter.

"I have no doubt a visit to Paradise Valley would be very enjoyable, captain," she replied, with a smile, "that is, if the place is at all suggestive of the name, but like your daughters, I shall be perfectly contented whether we stop there for a time or go on directly home."

"There!" exclaimed Rosie, "were ever such accommodating girls seen before? Now, Brother Levis, when I am asked that question I shall give a different reply, if only to furnish a trifle of the spice of variety."

"Consider it asked then, my dear young

sister," he returned, with assumed gravity, but a twinkle of fun in his eye.

"I do, and my answer is, that I am decidedly in favor of accepting Cousin Molly's invitation. I have a great desire to see Paradise, since the thing may be so easily accomplished, and nobody seems to have any objection to going there."

"Then we will consider the question decided in the affirmative," said the captain, "and make our arrangements accordingly."

"Not allowing among them an avoidance of Quebec, I trust," said Walter; "for I own that I very much want to see that old city."

"Set your mind at rest on that point, my boy," said the captain pleasantly; "I hardly think there is one of us who would willingly miss that visit."

"I am glad to hear you say that, captain," said Evelyn, "for I, for one, am looking forward to our visit there with a great deal of interest."

The little ones now asked to be excused, and went away to their plays, but the others sat about the table reading their letters—now and then a few sentences aloud, for the benefit of the company—until Walter had finished his meal, when they all gathered in the saloon for their regular morning service of prayer, Bible reading, and sacred song.

When that duty had been duly attended to, the gentlemen and some of the ladies went upon deck for a time. Rain was still falling, but less heavily than in the earlier hours, and Captain Raymond and Mr. Dinsmore decided to pay a visit to the city, promising to return in an hour or two, bringing vehicles for a drive, in case the weather should so improve that a little excursion might be taken with safety and pleasure.

Mrs. Travilla, Violet, and the young girls and Walter stood upon the deck, watching their departure.

"I hope they may enjoy themselves, but I shouldn't like to walk out in this drizzle" sighed Grace. Then in a lower, livelier tone, "Mamma, are you not proud of your husband? I think he is very handsome, even in that unbecoming waterproof coat."

"And I am decidedly of the opinion that everything becomes him," returned Violet, with a low, pleased laugh. "Well, mamma and you girls, how shall we pass the morning? It really seems to me that the saloon is more inviting and comfortable at present than the deck."

The others agreed with her, and all went below, where they found the two little ones begging Grandma Rose for a story to while away the time.

"Ah," she said, "here comes your Grandma
Elsie, who is far better than I am at that
business.

"Oh, yes!" cried little Elsie. "Grandma,
won't you please tell us now about things that
have happened at Montreal and Quebec?"

"Yes, dear; I promised you, and there will
be no better time than this for the telling of
the story," Mrs. Travilla answered pleasantly,
as she seated herself and took up her fancy
work, while the children drew their chairs to her
side, each young face full of eager expectancy.

CHAPTER XI.

GRANDMA ELSIE took a moment to collect her thoughts, then gave the little ones very much the same story of the settlement and after-history of Montreal that Lucilla had heard from their father earlier in the day. From that she went on to give a similar account of Quebec.

"The city," she said, "is built upon a steep promontory, where two rivers, the St. Lawrence, on which we now are, and the St. Charles meet. There was formerly an Indian village there called Stadacona. Jacques Cartier, the same person I have been telling you about as the first white man who visited this spot where Montreal now stands, discovered that Indian village in the same year. But the city of Quebec was not founded until 1608; and not by Cartier, but by another man named Champlain, who on the third day of July of that year raised over it a white flag. Soon afterward rude cottages were built, a few acres of ground cleared, and one or two gardens were planted."

"Is that all of it there is now, grandma?" asked Elsie.

"Oh, no, my child! there is a city with a very strong fortress; there are colleges and churches; there is a building yard for vessels, where thirty or forty are built every year. Quebec has a very fine harbor, where many vessels can ride at anchor at the same time, and I have read that from fourteen hundred to two thousand come in every year from the ocean."

"Just to ride there, grandma?" asked Neddie, with grave earnestness. Then he wondered why grandma smiled at his query and everybody else laughed.

"No, sonnie," Mrs. Travilla replied, "but to trade. They bring goods to the people—silk, cotton, woolen; salt too, coal, and hardware. And they carry away what the folks in Canada have to sell, which is mostly timber."

"Did you say French folks live there, grandma?" asked Elsie.

"Yes; it was built by the French in the first place, but taken from them by the English in 1759."

"That was before our Revolution, wasn't it, grandma?"

"Yes; about sixteen years earlier."

"Please tell about it, grandma."

Grandma kindly complied.

"There was war at that time between England and France," she said, "and, for that reason, war between the English and French colonies of America. The French built a strong fortress on the island of Cape Breton, which is at the mouth of this, the St. Lawrence River; they began also to build forts along the lakes and the Ohio and Mississippi Rivers. Fleets and armies came over from Europe, and the English and French colonists, on this side of the ocean, formed armies and engaged Indians to help them fight each other. The English attacked the French fortress of Louisburgh on Cape Breton Island, and took it. Then Wolfe, who was in command, put his troops on board of vessels, and went on up the river as far as the island of Orleans, a few miles below Quebec. There they built batteries for guns, intending to fire upon Quebec, where was the French general, Montcalm, with an army of 13,000 men; some of them regulars, the rest Canadians and Indians.

"But I will not go into all the particulars, as you two little ones could hardly understand them well enough to be much interested."

"Oh, yes, grandma, please go on," exclaimed Elsie.

"The English were unsuccessful at first, if

I remember right, mamma?" remarked Rosie inquiringly.

"Yes," replied her mother. "It was nearly night when their divisions joined, and the grenadiers were so impatient that they charged madly upon the works of the French before the other troops had time to form and be ready to sustain them. As a natural consequence they were driven back to the beach with severe loss, where they sought shelter behind a redoubt abandoned by the French.

"A storm was brewing, and the French kept up a galling fire, until it burst upon their foes with great fury. The tide from the ocean came roaring up against the current of the river with unusual strength, and the British were obliged to retreat to their camp across the Montmorency, to avoid being caught in the raging waters and drowned. They had lost 180 killed and 650 wounded.

"Wolfe, who was not a strong, healthy man, was so distressed over the calamity that he became really ill. Of course he was much fatigued, and that, joined to distress of mind, brought on a fever and other illness that nearly cost him his life. It was almost a month before he was able to resume command.

"When sufficiently recovered to write a letter, he sent an almost despairing one to Pitt, but at its close said he would do his best. Then he and Admiral Saunders contrived their plan for scaling the Heights of Abraham, and so getting possession of the elevated plateau at the back of the city, where the fortifications were weakest, the French engineers having trusted for their defence to the precipices and the river below.

"Montcalm and his men saw that the English camp was broken up, and that the troops were conveyed across to Point Levi, then some distance up the river, by a part of their fleet, while the rest of it remained behind to feign an attack upon the intrenchment at Beauport. Montcalm, though he saw these movements, was at a loss to understand them; so he remained in his camp, while another officer was stationed a little above the Plains of Abraham, to watch that part of the English fleet that had sailed up the river.

"At night the troops were all embarked in flat boats and proceeded up the river with the tide. The French saw them, and marched up the shore to prevent them from landing. Toward daylight the boats moved cautiously down the river, with muffled oars, passing the French without being perceived, and the troops landed safely in a cove below. They were all on shore by daylight.

"Then the light infantry scrambled up the precipice and dispersed a French guard stationed there, while the rest of the army climbed up a winding and steep ravine. Then another division landed, and before sunrise five thousand British troops were drawn up in battle array on the Plains of Abraham, three hundred feet above the St. Lawrence."

"How surprised the French must have been!" exclaimed Lucilla.

"Yes," said Mrs. Travilla, "the first intimation Montcalm had of their intentions was the sight of the English army drawn up there, on what he had doubtless deemed those inaccessible heights. He at once perceived that this exposed his garrison and the city to imminent danger, and immediately marched his whole army across the St. Charles to attack the enemy.

"It was about ten o'clock when he got his troops there and into battle line. He had two field-pieces, while the English had but one; only a light six-pounder which some sailors had dragged up the ravine about eight o'clock that morning.

"At that time the plains had no fences or inclosures, and extended to the walls of the city on the St. Louis side, their surface being dotted over with bushes which furnished places of

concealment for the French and Indian marks-
men. I will not attempt to describe the rela-
tive positions of the two armies, which you
little ones would hardly understand. I will
only say that Wolfe placed himself on the
right, at the head of a regiment of grenadiers
who were burning to avenge their defeat at
the Montmorency, and Montcalm was on the
left of the French, at the head of his regiments.

"Wolfe ordered his men to load their pieces
with two bullets each and reserve their fire
until the French should be within forty yards
of them, an order which every man was careful to obey.

"The English fired several rounds, then
charged furiously with their bayonets. Wolfe
was urging them on, when some Canadians
singled him out and fired, slightly wounding
him in the wrist. He wound his handkerchief
about it and still went on, cheering his men, but
quickly received another wound in the groin;
then another struck him in the breast, and he
fell to the ground mortally wounded. But he
seemed hardly to think of himself, only of his
troops and gaining the victory. 'Support me;
let not my brave soldiers see me drop,' he said
to an officer near him. 'The day is ours—keep
it.' Then they carried him to the rear while
his troops were still charging. The officer on

whose shoulder he was leaning cried out, 'They run, they run!' At that the light came back into the dim eyes of the dying hero and he asked, 'Who run?' 'The enemy, sir; they give way everywhere,' replied the officer. 'What! do they run already?' asked the feeble, dying voice. 'Go to Colonel Preston and tell him to march Webb's regiment immed'ately to the bridge over the St. Charles, and cut off the fugitives' retreat. Now, God be praised, I die happy!' He spoke no more, but died, with his sorrowing companions about him, just in the moment of victory. Montcalm too was mortally wounded in that battle, and died the next morning about five o'clock."

"What a pity!" exclaimed little Ned. "What makes men fight so, grandma?"

"If there were no sin there would be no fighting," Grandma Elsie replied. "There is none in heaven; there all is peace and joy and love."

"Is it bad men that fight, grandma?"

"Not quite always; sometimes a good man has to fight to protect his wife and children, or other helpless ones, from being injured by a bad man. If a bad man were trying to hurt your mamma, or one of your sisters, it would be right for your papa to prevent him, even if he had to hurt him a great deal in doing so."

"Oh, yes; and when I grow big I won't let anybody hurt my dear mamma or sisters. I'll help papa drive 'em away if they try to."

"Please, grandma, tell some more," entreated Elsie.

"Yes, dear," said grandma. "The British have kept Quebec ever since they took it that time, and there was no more fighting there till our Revolutionary war began some sixteen years later: the 19th of April, 1775. In the fall of that year troops were sent to Canada; some under Ethan Allen, as you have already learned, some under Montgomery, and others commanded by Arnold.

"They, poor fellows, had dreadful times pushing their way through the wilderness, often suffering for lack of sufficient food and raiment, braving storms and bitter cold. I cannot tell you the whole sad story now, but you can read it when you are older. Arnold and his men reached Quebec first, but were not strong enough to attack it, and the garrison would not come out and fight them on the plains. Then Arnold, inspecting his arms, found that most of his cartridges were spoiled, therefore he retreated to a place twenty miles distant. There, on the 1st of December, he was joined by Montgomery and his troops; but very few of them were fit for fighting,

many being sick; also a good many had
deserted, so that the force was small indeed—
only about nine hundred men."

"What's desert, grandma, to run away
without leave?" asked Neddie.

"Yes," she replied; "and they generally
shoot a soldier for it."

"I think I won't be a soldier when I get big,"
said the little fellow reflectively; "'cause I
might get scared and run away and the other
fellows might catch me and shoot me; and
then papa and mamma would feel very sorry;
wouldn't they, grandma?"

"Yes, indeed! and so would a good many
other folks, grandma for one," she replied,
dropping her work to put an arm about him,
stroking his hair with the other hand, patting
his rosy cheek, and kissing him again and
again. "But we hope our little boy will make a
good and brave man, like his father, and never
play the coward by running away from dangerous duty."

"Maxie, my big brother, wouldn't, grandma."

"No, I feel very sure Max would fight for
the right and his dear native land."

"So do I," said Lucilla. "Max is very much
like our father in both looks and character;
though papa says Max has a better temper than
his. I never saw papa show a bad temper, but

he says he has one and that that's where I get mine."

"Now, Lu, don't talk in that way about yourself," said Grace. "I've hardly seen you show any temper at all for years past. If you got it from papa, you got the power of controlling it too, from him, I think."

At that moment Walter came hurrying down from the deck, whither he had gone shortly before, his face full of joyous excitement.

"Folks," he cried, "do you know that it is clearing off? The sun is out and the clouds are retreating rapidly before it. Surely the change will bring grandpa and the captain back in haste, after the rest of us. So I think we should better be making our preparations as fast as possible."

"Why, my dear young brother," laughed Rosie, "one would imagine our lives or fortunes, one or both, depended on our seeing the sights of Montreal to-day."

"Very well, my wise sister, you can stay behind, if you wish," laughed the lad; "but I'm bound to make one of the exploring party. And there! they have come, for I hear Brother Levis' voice on deck."

The words had scarcely left his lips when Captain Raymond's quick, manly step was heard coming down the companion-way; then his pleasant voice, saying, "Everybody who wants to see Montreal to-day must make haste to don hat and coat or shawl, for the air will be quite cool in driving."

"Oh, have you brought a carriage for us, papa?" asked little Elsie.

"Yes," he replied; "we have three of what they call *calèches* out here on the wharf. They are pleasant vehicles to ride in, and the three will hold us all very comfortably. We will not want to stop anywhere for dinner," he continued turning to Violet, "so I have ordered a lunch put up for each *calèche*."

"My dear, you think of everything," she said, with an admiring affectionate look up into his face. "We will be ready in ten minutes; we need no preparations but what you have advised."

CHAPTER XII.

THE sun had already set when our friends returned to the *Dolphin*. They had greatly enjoyed their drive and the views of the places of interest visited, but were weary enough to be glad to find themselves again seated upon the deck of their floating home. The little ones were given a simple meal and sent to their berths, then the elder people sat down to a more substantial one, over which they chatted and laughed, discussing with much enjoyment the sights of the day and the historical events with which they were connected.

Then they talked of Quebec and upon what parts of it they should bestow most attention, as they could tarry there for but a short time.

"Of course we must visit the Heights of Abraham, whatever else we neglect," remarked Rosie.

"Yes," said Walter, "and Palace Gate, Cape Diamond, and the citadel that crowns it. I should like to see it, not only for the historical associations, but also because it is said to be the most impregnable fortress on the continent of America."

"And I, for the beautiful view it commands of what is called the most magnificent scenery on this continent, if not in the world," added Violet.

"It must be very large," remarked Lucilla, "for I remember reading that, with its ravelins, it covers about forty acres. We will go to see it, papa, will we not?"

"I think so; it would hardly do to visit Quebec and neglect so important a place."

"It was under Cape Diamond that Montgomery fell, if I remember right," remarked Evelyn Leland.

"Yes," replied the captain; "on the 31st of December, 1775. At two o'clock on that morning his troops paraded in three divisions; a part at Holland House under the direct command of Montgomery. That division, with Montgomery at the head, passed down from the Plains of Abraham to Wolf's Cove, then along the margin of the river under Cape Diamond. It was a dark, stormy morning, the snow falling fast and a fierce wind piling it in heaps—frightful drifts. Through that darkness and storm Montgomery led his men to the narrowest point under the cape, where, on the top of the precipice, the enemy had planted a battery of three-pounders. The post was in charge of a Canadian with thirty-eight militiamen, besides nine British seamen under the master of a transport, to work the guns. These men were awake and on the watch, perfectly silent; each artilleryman with a lighted match in his hand. Probably from their silence Montgomery thought they were asleep. But they were waiting and listening.

"Barnsfare could see faintly through the dim light and drifting snow, the movements of the Americans, and when they drew near, and Montgomery called out to his troops, 'Men of New York, you will not fear to follow where your general leads: March on!' rushing, as he spoke, over heaps of snow and ice to charge the battery. Barnsfare heard, gave his men the word, and they sent a discharge of grape-shot, sweeping down the American ranks with terrible effect.

"Montgomery, his aid, Major M'Phunn, Captain Cheesman, and several privates were killed, and the rest, appalled at the disaster and the death of their brave commander, fled back to Wolf's Cove."

"How dreadful!" sighed Grace. "Montgomery's death alone was a great loss to our country, was it not, papa?"

"It was indeed! throughout the whole

country his death was felt to be a great calamity, and even in England, upon the floor of Parliament, his praises were sounded by Burke, Chatham, and Barre."

"Was he buried there—in Canada?" she asked.

"Yes; within the wall that surrounded a powder magazine, near the ramparts on St. Louis Street. There his body remained for forty-two years, when it was removed to New York and reinterred near the monument erected to his memory by the United States.

"While all this was going on at Cape Diamond, Arnold and his division were passing along the St. Charles. The snow was worse drifted there than on the St. Lawrence; but he and his men pressed on till they reached a narrow street, where, under a high jutting rock, the enemy had a two-gun picketed battery well manned. Like Montgomery he headed his men, leading Lamb's artillery to the attack, and while doing so received a very bad wound in the knee. He had to be carried to the general hospital, and there heard the sad news of Montgomery's death.

"Morgan now took command of Arnold's division, and for more than an hour the Americans withstood the storm of musket balls and grape-shot at the first barrier, and finally carried

it, the deadly aim of the riflemen causing great
consternation among the ranks of the British
and Canadians. Then they rushed on to the
second, where they fought fiercely for three
hours, many being killed on both sides.

"Our men finally captured the barrier, and
were preparing to rush into the town, when
Carleton sent a large detachment from his garrison, through Palace Gate, to attack them in
the rear. He and his men had heard of the
death of Montgomery and the retreat of his
detachment, which inspired them with renewed
courage. The Palace Gate was thrown open
suddenly and the troops rushed out, surprising
Captain Dearborn and some provincials stationed there, and they were taken prisoners.

"Morgan heard of that disaster and of the
death of Montgomery while he and his men
were pressing on vigorously into the town;
also that the enemy was advancing on his rear.
He saw that further efforts were useless, as he
was surrounded by the foe on all sides, and he
and his men surrendered themselves prisoners
of war."

"The whole American army was not taken,
if I remember right, papa?" said Grace inter-
rogatively.

"No," replied her father, "the rest of the
division retreated to their camp, leaving

behind a field-piece and some mortars. Colonel Arnold took command of what was left of the patriot army and was promoted to the rank of brigadier-general. He did not feel safe so near the city, so retired about three miles from it and intrenched himself as well as circumstances would permit. He remained there until the 1st of April, but accomplished nothing of any consequence. General Thomas, who was appointed to succeed Montgomery, arrived early in May; but the British received large reinforcements and our men were driven out of Canada."

"Perhaps it was just as well," remarked Lucilla, in a tone of indifference, "our country is large enough, and I, for one, don't covet Canada."

"I think there are very few Americans, if any, who do," returned her father with a slightly amused smile. "Our country is large enough, and while we like the Canadians as friends and neighbors, we have no wish to change their political relations, or to rob England of her colonies."

"I think you are quite correct about that matter, captain," said Mr. Dinsmore. "I have yet to hear from any one of our people an expression of a desire to see Canada, or any part of British America, incorporated into our

Union. We have a great country and are fully satisfied with its size."

"'Eternal vigilance is the price of liberty,'" quoted Walter, "and we need to be careful to exercise that, don't we, grandpa?"

"Certainly we do," was the reply, "toward foes within and foes without; and that especially by diffusing knowledge and teaching Gospel truth."

With that they withdrew from the table and gathered upon the deck. The yacht was moving down the river, but through the gathering gloom little could be seen of it or its shores, and wearied with the day's jaunt, all presently retired to their staterooms.

CHAPTER XIII.

WHEN the *Dolphin's* passengers awoke the next morning they found she had reached Quebec and was lying quietly at the wharf there. Anxious to view all places of historic interest in and about the city and to be again on their eastward way, they set out as promptly as they conveniently could after leaving the breakfast table.

There were so many points of interest, and at some they tarried so long, that the sun had set and shadows were already creeping over land and water as they regained the *Dolphin's* deck.

Ned was fast asleep in his father's arms, little Elsie hardly able to keep her eyes open, and they were taken at once to their stateroom by their parents, the others hurrying to theirs to make due preparation for a suitable appearance at the supper table.

The saloon through which they passed was but dimly lighted as yet, and no one noticed a lady and gentleman sitting side by side in a far corner where the shadows were deepest.

As the last stateroom door closed upon its occupants, the gentleman leaned down over the lady, saying in a tone scarcely above a whisper, "Ah ha, ah ha, um h'm! they are all safe in their rooms for the present, and now let us go upon deck while we may unperceived. Raymond will be sure to be up there presently, if none o' the rest."

The lady returned a silent assent, both rose, crossed the room noiselessly, ascended the cabin stairway, and in another minute were seated side by side in the shadow of the pilot house, the man at the wheel greeting them with a quiet smile of amusement.

"They didn't see you, sir?" he asked in an undertone.

"No. And you kept our counsel?"

"An easy thing to do under the circumstances, as the captain asked no question, but passed quickly on down into the cabin. But I think, sir, you'd best let him know you're here pretty soon, or the yacht may be starting with you and the lady on it, and you haven't any baggage aboard."

"That's true; but the captain shall know of our presence and give us time to land before he weighs anchor."

"And here he comes now, sir," as at that moment Captain Raymond's step and voice were heard near the companion-way. "There, do you hear, sir? he's giving the order to weigh anchor and proceed down the river."

"Hallo, there, cap'in! jest you wait a bit, sir. There's a couple o' stowaways aboard and I'd advise ye to get rid o' them afore ye start," called a voice that seemed to come from some part of the vessel in the captain's rear.

He turned quickly, asking, "And you are one of them?"

"Well, sir, that's neither here nor there," returned the voice; "but if I was in your place, I'd put 'em off afore starting."

"But perhaps the poor fellows need some help," returned the captain. "Tell them to show themselves and I'll not be hard upon them."

"Well, now," exclaimed the invisible speaker, "I must say you're a good, kind-hearted sort o' man, spite o' owning this grand yacht and a lot o' money, so I'll call 'em. Halloo, here, mates, don't be afeard to show yerselves and I reckon ye'll git some grub if nuthin' else."

"Wait a little till this matter is settled," Captain Raymond said, reversing his order about the anchor, then asked, "Have any strangers been allowed to board the yacht during my absence?" addressing his query to the man at the helm.

"Well, no, sir; not to say strangers," answered the man, hesitatingly and with a slight laugh.

"Ah! some old friends, though; just as I suspected," and with the words Captain Raymond glanced searchingly about, then with a quick step drew near the hiding place of the stowaways.

"Ah, cousins, I see my guess was not wide of the mark," he said, with his good-humored laugh and giving a hand to each. "You are as welcome as sunlight in the morning and shall have all the 'grub' you can stow away. But why not send for your baggage and go on home with us? You have seen all the sights of Quebec, have you not?"

"About all, captain," replied Mr. Lilburn, "and we thank you heartily for your very kind invitation. But though travel on the *Dolphin*, especially in such good company, is most delightful, we would crowd you too much, I fear."

"Yes," said Annis, "and it would be very selfish to give ourselves so much pleasure at the cost of such inconvenience to our kind friends—our dear relatives. But seeing the *Dolphin* lying here, we felt that we could not deny ourselves the great pleasure of a peep at you all."

"The voyage is not likely to be a long one,

or the crowding worth mentioning," returned
Captain Raymond in his most cordial tone;
"and the slight inconvenience will be paid for
over and over again by the pleasure of your
company."

"It is most kind in you to say so, captain,"
said Annis, with a pleased look, "but are you
quite sure the others would be equally willing
to endure the inconvenience?"

"I haven't a doubt of it," he replied emphatically, "and I know of nothing that could
happen just now that would afford our dear
mother more pleasure; for I have often heard
her speak of you as her very dear friend and
cousin, and I know she has missed you sadly
since you left us for your bridal trip. If you
have seen all you care to of the city, do let me
send at once for your baggage and give her
and the rest the pleasant surprise of finding you
presently at the supper table."

"Thank you very much," she said, smiling
up into his pleasant face; "you don't know
how tempting your kind offer is. We have
seen all we care to of this interesting old city
and were intending to leave it to-night;
but——"

"Ah, my dear cousin, just omit the objec-
tions," interrupted Captain Raymond laughingly, "give me the address and let me send at

once for your trunks. Excuse my rudeness in not waiting to hear all you could say against my plan, but it is growing late and I can hear it all afterward if you care to have me do so. Ah, here comes mother and my wife now," he added, as the two stepped upon the deck at that moment.

Then moving quickly toward them, "I have something to show you, mother and Vi," he said; "a couple of uncommonly interesting stowaways, about the disposal of whom I should like to have your advice."

"Stowaways?" repeated Violet, in accents of surprise. "Do they think we are about to cross the ocean?"

"Suppose you come and have a little talk with them," said her husband, leading the way toward the intruders, the ladies following close in his rear.

"Oh, Cousins Annis and Ronald! How delightful!" both exclaimed at sight of the intruders, Vi adding in gleeful tones, "We'll stow you away safely and keep you as long as possible."

Then, as Annis began repeating her objection on the score of the inevitable crowding, "Oh, that will only be fun," she said. "I am not urging you out of politeness, but because I really want your and Cousin Ronald's pleasant company, and know that all the rest will be delighted to have it."

"Certainly they will," added Grandma Elsie. "And you surely cannot be so unkind, Annis dear, as to refuse us that pleasure."

"Ah, Annis, my bonny bride, with such assurances we need not hesitate," laughed Mr. Lilburn. "Let us accept the kind invitation and do our best to add to the pleasure of our generous-hearted entertainers."

"You can hardly refuse to follow such good advice coming from such a source, Annis," said Violet, while Captain Raymond again inquired of Mr. Lilburn where he should send for the trunks.

The requested information was given, a messenger at once despatched for the luggage, and, as the summons to the supper table came at the same moment, all the company upon the deck at once descended the companion-way and met the remainder of the family party at the table. The bride and groom had no reason to complain of their reception, for everyone seemed delighted to see them.

Fatigue was forgotten in the enjoyment of each other's society, the toothsome viands and the interest of comparing notes as to their experiences—all they had seen, heard, and done —since the parting of a few days before, when the bride and groom left the *Dolphin* for the railroad train at Michigan City.

The luggage had arrived and the vessel was in motion down the river some time before they left the table.

"You will hardly make another stop in this part of Her Majesty's dominions, captain, but go directly home, I presume?" remarked Mr. Lilburn inquiringly, at a pause in the conversation.

"Yes and no," returned Captain Raymond in playful tones, "I hardly expect to stop again until we reach Narragansett Bay; but there we expect to visit Newport, and Paradise Valley, a few miles out of it, on the same island. We have some cousins summering there now, who are most urgent with us to come and take temporary possession of a vacant cottage very near the one occupied by them; and we have decided to do so, should nothing interfere. And now, I hope you and Cousin Annis will decide to go there with us, and afterward return home with us in the *Dolphin.*"

As soon as the captain had ceased speaking, Mrs. Travilla and Violet, the young people also, joined their urgent solicitations to his, and as Annis seemed much pleased with the idea, and Mr. Lilburn himself had really no objection, it was presently decided that they would accept the invitation.

They now left the table and gathered upon the deck for a time; but as there was no moon that night little could be seen of the country through which they were passing, and all being somewhat weary with the exertions of the day, they presently held their regular evening service of prayer, praise, and reading of the Scriptures, then bade an affectionate good-night and retired to rest.

CHAPTER XIV.

Our friends had a delightful voyage through the Gulf of St. Lawrence, down the coasts of New Brunswick, Maine, Massachusetts, and Rhode Island as far as Newport on Narragansett Bay. They left the yacht lying in the harbor there for the present, and taking hired carriages drove out to the cottages of which their cousin, Mrs. Embury, had written, where they found her and Mr. Embury, with their children, also Mr. and Mrs. Cyril Keith, forming a large and interesting family party, and filling one of the cottages; but the other was still vacant, and large enough to accommodate very conveniently the entire party from the *Dolphin*.

Their welcome was of the warmest. They found their new temporary abode comfortably, though not elegantly, furnished, open and well aired; for, though their friends had been uncertain of the exact time of their arrival, they had expected them daily and made ready, as far as possible, for their comfort and enjoyment.

"Ah, if we had only known just when you would get here, your supper should have been ready," said Isadore, when greetings had been exchanged and the excitement of the arrival had calmed down somewhat. "But I will have it on the table as soon as possible. I am house-keeper this week. Molly and I take the position week about, each trying to outdo the other in catering for the united family."

"Oh, thank you! but we had supper on the yacht just before leaving her," said Violet. "Besides, we consider ourselves at home and do not expect or wish to be treated as company."

"And we have brought a supply of pro-visions of various kinds, which we hope you may be willing to share with us," said the captain.

"That was very kind and thoughtful in you, cousin captain," returned Isadore with a pleased look, "and I hardly think any of us will feel inclined to reject your dainties; though we have fared very well indeed since coming here."

"Please accept my thanks also, and those of our husbands and children," said Molly. "Aunt Rose and Cousin Elsie, please sit down here with the gentlemen and let us younger ones attend to the unpacking and arranging of the contents of your trunks. If you will trust us, I can assure you we shall enjoy doing it. At least I am sure I shall."

"That is a kind offer, Molly," said Mrs. Travilla, "but we have done nothing to-day to tire us and I, for one, am not in the least fatigued; so ought not to indulge my love of ease at your expense."

"Your love of ease, Cousin Elsie!" laughed Molly. "I never discovered that you had any."

"No; but she has a daughter who is both able and willing to attend to the duty in question," said Rosie Travilla. "So sit you down, mother dear, and enjoy this pleasant company, while we younger folks unpack and find places for your goods and chattels."

"Yes, do, mother," said Captain Raymond, bringing forward an easy chair for her. "Can't you trust me to oversee and assist these younger folks? If not we will seat you in state in some spot convenient for you to do that part in person."

"Thanks, captain," she returned with a smile of amusement "as commanding and giving directions has been your business for so many years, I think you may be trusted to attend to the matter even without my added supervision."

"Yes, come along, sir," said Rosie, leading

the way, "but please to remember that you and we girls are not in the schoolroom."

"I shall endeavor to keep that fact in mind, my sage young sister," he said in return.

"But it won't make any difference in your authority over your own daughters, I am happy to know, papa," Lucilla said, with a loving, smiling look up into his face.

"No; they are mine and under my orders always and under all circumstances," he returned; "and I think would not have it other wise if they might."

"Indeed we would not," said Grace, who, as usual, was near her father and sister. "May I help, papa?"

"Well, Gracie, I think you are not really needed, and would enjoy yourself better out yonder on the porches or on the grass with your little brother and sister and the others, telling them stories, singing them little songs or playing games with them."

"Yes; do try that, Gracie, and I shall be much obliged," Violet said, joining them at the moment. "I have just left them with the promise to ask it of you."

Grace acquiesced, went back at once, and for the next half hour devoted herself to the amusement of the children, to their great satisfaction and enjoyment.

"And you, Madam Raymond, would do well to go back to the society of your older friends and exercise your many gifts for their entertainment," remarked the captain, speaking in playful tones to his young wife, as Grace disappeared.

"No, my dear, I prefer to exercise them for yours, if you will permit it," she returned.

"Ah, you fear to trust me to do the work without the supervision of my capable young wife?" he returned laughingly.

"Possibly it may be done a trifle better, or, at least, more to my mind, with that," she retorted, with becoming gravity. "At all events, I shall know better where to look for what I want, so that, in the end, I shall save myself trouble."

"Ah, then, I will make no further objection, but freely acknowledge that the work will be twice as enjoyable if done under my young wife's supervision."

"Thank you, sir," laughed Violet; "How glad I am now that I insisted on coming to share it. As our stay is likely to be so short, I think, do not you, it will be best to unpack only such things as we are pretty sure to want while here?"

"Very well, my dear; as concerns that matter, you have only to give your orders and see them carried out; while I do likewise in regard to another; namely, that all the manual labor is to be left to other hands than yours."

"Oh, Captain Raymond, how you do spoil me!" laughed Violet. "Who shall say that you won't be sorry for it one of these days, and wish you had encouraged me to be industrious and energetic."

"I am willing to take the risk," he said, placing a chair for her.

"No, I am not ready to sit down yet," she said. "We must first settle who are to be the occupants of each room; and Cousin Annis and Ronald should have the first choice."

"Decidedly they must have of the best; yet, I think it may be the better plan for us to choose for them, or they will not take the best. There are three comfortable rooms on this first floor. Shall we not assign their use to your mother, grandparents, and the Lilburn cousins?"

"By all means," returned Violet. "Then Rosie will share with mamma, Evelyn and our two girls take one of the third story rooms, you and I and our little ones another, and Walter the remaining one. He, you know, must leave us in a few days for college. Oh, the house will accommodate us all very nicely!"

"So I think," he returned, leading the way

to the third story; "and now I insist on your having the first choice of the rooms on this floor."

Violet hesitated, glancing inquiringly at Evelyn and Lucilla, who had followed them up the stairway.

"Yes, Cousin Vi, that is only right, and what we would prefer to have you do," said Evelyn.

"I see hardly any choice; they all look pleasant," added Lucilla, "and if there is a difference, of course, we would all prefer that you and papa should have the best."

Violet still seemed to hesitate, and Walter, who had come up in the rear of the others, said, "I see I'll have to decide this knotty question. My big brother, the captain, being the largest, oldest, best, and most distinguished of this party, besides having a better half and two children to share with him, should be assigned the largest room; the three young ladies should take the next in size, and I—'lone and lorn' bachelor of sixteen—will occupy the smallest, which is quite large enough and good enough for me. So there the knotty question is solved."

"Many thanks for your wise decision, my dear young bachelor brother," laughed Violet. "And now, if you and your big brother will see to the bringing up of the trunks, I think we will

soon make an end of unpacking and arranging
their contents, and be ready to join the pleasant
company on the porches."

"Yes, I think we need not do much of that
work to-night," said her husband; "it is now
almost time to get our little ones to bed, and
to-morrow will give us another and better opportunity."

With that he and Walter hastened down the
stairway, and not many minutes later all were
ready to rejoin the friends and relatives sitting
at ease on the porches below.

Most of the evening was passed in conversation, for they found a great deal to hear and to
tell of the scenes they had visited, and occurrences in the family connection since last they
had been together.

They had been talking of Viamede, Mrs.
Travilla asking some questions of Mr. Cyril
Keith about the condition of things there, of
which he was able to render a very favorable
report, in which Mr. Lilburn, among others,
seemed to be much interested.

"You visited Viamede some time ago, I remember, sir?" remarked Cyril, turning to him.

"Yes; some few years ago, and found it a
lovely place—a sort of earthly paradise," returned the old gentleman, adding, with a look
of amusement, "I am pleased to perceive that

you have not forgotten me entirely, though we were not, at that time, related by marriage as we are now. I have no objection in the world to being called uncle, even by a man of your age, seeing you are own nephew to my bonny young wife."

Annis laughed, saying with a mirthful look, "Hardly young to anyone but yourself, my dear; only a trifle younger than my dear friend and cousin Elsie, who is grandmother to quite a number of fine children."

"But still almost youthful in appearance, auntie, dear," said Cyril, giving Mrs. Travilla a look of heart-felt affection. Then turning to Mr. Lilburn, "I shall avail myself in the future of the privilege you have accorded me, Uncle Ronald," he said. "It is a pleasant name to speak, and a dear old gentleman who gives me the privilege of so addressing him."

"Couldn't you give us all the same privilege, sir?" asked Mr. Embury. "My wife is own cousin to your new niece, Mrs. Isadore Keith— I think, too, that she is the bright, attractive sort of woman anybody might be proud to claim kin with—and we would all feel just so about claiming it with you. Besides that, Uncle Ronald is a good, agreeable, handy name to use and to hear."

"Ah ha! ah ha! um h'm! so I think myself;

also that this is a handy company to own as nieces and nephews. But what say you, Annis, my bonny bride?" turning to her, with a look that spoke proud ownership.

"That I am entirely willing you should be uncle and I aunt to the whole crowd of good people here, if they desire it," Annis answered, with a look of amusement. "It will not make us really any older in feeling or appearance. And I am quite accustomed to having nieces and nephews not very many years younger than myself."

"And have not found it a nearly unendurable trial, I hope, Aunt Annis?" Cyril said inquiringly.

"No; quite the contrary," she answered. "But, to change the subject; there is a good deal that is interesting to be seen about here, is there not?"

"Yes, indeed! This is Middletown; it was formerly a part of Newport, and known in those times as 'ye woods.' It has an area of twelve and a half square miles. There are five schoolhouses, three churches, and a town hall."

"Why, I thought it was country!" exclaimed Rosie. "As we drove along I noticed little groups of houses here and there, but there seemed to be farms, orchards, and fields; also a good many rocky-looking hills; some that didn't seem to be cultivated at all."

"Yet, there is so much beauty that it seems to me worthy of its name—Paradise Valley," remarked her mother.

"I think so," said Cyril, "and I expect to enjoy taking you all to its various places of interest—Purgatory Rocks, Sachuest and Easton's Beaches, Hanging Rocks, and the site of the former residence of Bishop Berkeley."

"Who was he?" asked Grace.

"A clergyman, born in Ireland, educated in England; a learned man and author of a number of books; a good Christian man too; one of whose projects was the founding of a college in the Bermudas for the training of ministers to supply churches and teach Christianity to the savages of America. The English government was to supply the means, but failed to do so, and Berkeley came on here to Newport in January, 1729, bought a farm, built a small house upon it, and there lived and studied, preaching occasionally, while waiting for the performance of the promise of the English government. He waited about three years; then, convinced that the promise would never be kept, went back to England."

"And he left the income of his property

here to be used in educating students of **Yale**
College, did he not?" asked Violet.

"Yes; gave books too—a valuable collection
donated by himself and friends—and most of
the volumes are still there. He had a share in
the formation of Redwood Library here in
Newport, also. He was both a very good and
very distinguished man."

"Did he name this Paradise Valley?" asked
Grace.

"No, I have been told it was named by Mr.
Isaac Barker, who owned a large part, if not
all of it, in Revolutionary days. By the way,
his descendants still live here, one of them in
the very house owned and occupied by him at
that time."

"Oh, yes," said Molly; "we must take you
to see that house, so interesting because a relic
of the Revolution, and the dear old lady who is
now its mistress. I know you will be much interested in her, Cousin Elsie, and all she can tell
of events here in this valley during that war."

"I shall be glad to call to see her, if you are
quite sure she will not deem it an intrusion,"
replied Mrs. Travilla.

"No, I am sure she will not; she is very kind
and hospitable, and seems to really enjoy telling
the story of those times to one who shows a
deep interest in it."

"As we all would do," said Mr. Dinsmore, glancing at his watch as he spoke. "But it is growing late now. Shall we not have our evening worship together and then retire to rest? Cousin Cyril, as you are a minister, the rest only laymen, suppose you lead our devotions."

CHAPTER XV.

As they expected to make their stay upon the island but short, and wished to see every interesting spot, all were up and about early the next morning.

Naturally the history of the State, and particularly of the island upon which they were, was the principal topic of conversation at the breakfast table. Walter began it.

"If my memory serves me right, it was somewhere about here that General Nathaniel Greene had his quarters in 1778."

"Yes," replied Captain Raymond, "on a farm owned by Colonel Richard K. Randolph."

"Why, I thought Greene's fighting was done in other parts of the country!" said Rosie.

"Most of it was," replied the captain, "but being a Rhode Island man he desired to take a part in the attack on the British, who had possession of Newport at that time. But I think you all know the story—the failure of the French troops to take the part expected of them, and to do the damage to the British vessels coming in from New York which they essayed to do; then the great storm which damaged the vessels, both of the French and English; and, soon after, the sailing of the French for Boston, leaving the Americans to meet the British alone.

"Then the battle was fought on Quaker Hill, after which, though not defeated, the Americans, hearing of the approach of Howe with large reinforcements for the British, retreated from the island to the mainland, in good order and without the loss of a man."

"Did the British go away too, papa?" asked Elsie.

"Not till the fall of the next year," he replied. "They had done a vast amount of mischief, and desolated the island; they had cut down the groves of forest trees and many of the orchards, for fuel and military purposes; they had torn up the meadows, destroyed gardens and ruined farms. So hard had they made life upon the island that many, it is said more than half the people, had left the island; wharves were deserted, commerce was destroyed, and trade abandoned. In December of 1778, the last winter that they were there, there was a fearful storm—a heavy fall of snow and cold so intense that many of the Hessians perished, frozen to death. Accounts say that more than fifty people, mostly soldiers, lost their

lives on that fearful night, and it was long
known as the Hessian storm. The poor fellows
suffered very much that winter, for, after a
little, rations were cut down to one-half of bread,
made of rice and oatmeal mixed, the other half
of rice. And fuel was so scarce that they must
have suffered much from the cold; to supply it
old houses were destroyed, old wharves torn to
pieces. Old empty houses were used as barracks, and troops were quartered upon the
people still living in others. The State-house
was used as a hospital and some of the churches
were turned into riding-schools.

"General Prescott had his quarters in the
Bannister House, and it is said that his spacious
sidewalk in front was made of stepstones taken
from private houses, and the whole of the south
flight of steps from those belonging to the
State-house."

"I don't see in what respect he was any better
than a thief and a robber!" cried Lucilla indignantly.

"No, nor do I," said her father; "but we
must remember that some of the British officers
were a very different kind of men and would
not have at all approved of his doings. Prescott, as we all know, was a great coward, and
cowardice and cruelty are apt to go together."

"Our Washington was very, very brave and

never at all cruel," remarked little Elsie.
"Papa, was he ever here?"

"He was in Newport more than once. His
last visit was paid while he was President of
these United States in August, 1790. He was
escorted to the Brenton House, the principal
hotel of the place; a dinner was given him in
the representative chamber of the State-house,
at which thirteen regular toasts were drunk,
Washington giving one—'The town of Newport.' He left before the rest of the company,
and then Judge Marchant gave the toast, 'The
man we love.'"

"Oh, I like that!" said the little girl, her
eyes sparkling. "I think everybody must love
Washington—everybody but the British."

"And even some of the British have admired
him very much," said her father, smiling at her
enthusiasm.

"And given him high praise," added Walter.
"I for one am proud of being his countryman."

All had now finished their breakfast, and
leaving the table they repaired to the adjoin-
ing cottage, exchanged greetings with its occupants, then together they held their morning
service, after which they arranged their plans
for the day.

"As this is Saturday and I leave for Princeton on Tuesday next, I have only to-day and

Monday for looking about and seeing places of interest in this neighborhood," remarked Walter.

"How and where do you want to go?" asked Mr. Embury.

"Down to the beaches, to all the places connected with the doings of Bishop Berkeley and the Revolution, all about Paradise Valley, and—to look at Purgatory; but not to get into it," replied the lad, concluding with a slight laugh.

"Do you want company or prefer to go alone?" was the next query, to which Walter replied, "I can go alone, I suppose, but I should prefer good company if it is to be had."

"Would mine answer that description?"

"Yes, indeed, sir! but, I daresay, you have seen all the places already and perhaps might be only bored by being asked to repeat your visit."

"Quite a mistake, my young friend; they are worth looking at time and again."

"I should think so," remarked the captain. "Suppose we make up a party of such of our members as would enjoy a pretty long stroll, go down through this valley to the beach yonder, visit Purgatory Rocks and as many other of the places of interest as we may feel inclined to see to-day and have time and strength to visit."

"I approve of your plan," said Molly. "I was thinking it would be best to defer our intended visit to that dear old lady in the Revolutionary house till Monday, as Saturday is apt to be a busy one with housekeepers."

"Yes," said Mrs. Dinsmore, "I think it will be quite enough to venture an intrusion upon her at the most convenient time for her that we can select."

"A real favor for her to permit it at any time," added Grandma Elsie.

They were gathered on the porch. Captain Raymond now rose and looking down toward the water said, "Ah, yonder is the *Dolphin;* according to my order of yesterday she has been brought here to afford a sail along the coast of the island to any who may desire it."

"Oh, how good and kind in you, captain!" exclaimed Mrs. Keith. "I for one should be delighted to go."

"All can sail who wish," said the captain. "The *Dolphin* has day accommodations for even a larger company than this, and of course we shall return long before night."

As he concluded, he looked at Mrs. Dinsmore as if expecting her to speak first, and as she was the eldest lady in the company she did so, saying: "I for one have been so long on the water that I feel a strong inclination to stroll down to the beach; though I have no doubt that the sail will be very enjoyable."

"How would it do to take the stroll to the nearest point to where the yacht is lying, and then continue your walk, or go aboard the vessel, as you feel inclined?" asked the captain.

"Oh, nicely! I think," she returned; "especially if some of the others would like to join me in so doing."

"I should," "And I," "And I," cried several voices, one of them being Grandma Elsie's, and another Violet's; while at the same time nearly every one of the children was asking permission to go along.

"Yes, yes! let them all go," said the captain.

"A walk to the beach down yonder will not be too long for any one of them, I think, and when we get there each one of our party can decide whether to continue the stroll or board the yacht."

CHAPTER XVI.

"I THINK we will have to divide our forces," said Mr. Embury, when, after preliminary preparations and arrangements, all were ready to set out for the beach and the yacht, "for there are so many of us that we will astonish the natives and they will probably be asking the meaning and object of the procession."

"Well, my dear, what of what?" queried his wife gayly. "It will give them an interesting subject of inquiry and conversation."

"Very well, my Molly; if you like to be talked about, I have no further objection to make," was his cheerful response.

"There are a good many of us," remarked the captain, glancing about, "actually two dozen, counting all—big and little, old and young."

"And a very respectable-looking crowd it is," remarked Violet. "I'm not in the least ashamed of anyone in it. Yet it might be well to break up into several smaller parties, by the way of guarding against alarming our good neighbors, or making all the grown up ones keep to the slow pace of the very little folks. Ah, I see Evelyn, Rosie and Walter, Lu and Grace, are already on the wing."

"Yes," said the captain; "they have just started in response to a motion from me to move on. They will reach the beach probably some minutes ahead of us, but can be trusted not to get into any danger or mischief."

"Surely," laughed Violet. "Mamma, shall you and I walk together?"

"While I follow with the children," added the captain. "I see your grandpa and his wife are moving on ahead of us."

"Cousin Ronald should go next with his bonny bride, while we of this cottage bring up the rear with our children," said Molly.

"Putting a small space between to avoid being mistaken for a procession," added Mrs. Keith.

"Bound for Purgatory; but none of us to get inside, I trust," said Mr. Embury. "I hope the young folks won't attempt to climb up those rocks till we older ones get there to look after them."

"No, I think we'll find them on the beach," said the captain. "I bade mine wait there for me, and I can say—for mine, at least, that they love their father well enough to follow his directions carefully."

"That is very true," said Grandma Elsie; "and equally true with regard to the care with which my Rosie and Walter conform to mine."

"And no wonder, mamma and Levis," said Violet, "for you are both so reasonable in your commands and prohibitions, so kind and affectionate, that it would take a very hard-hearted and stubborn nature to rebel against your authority."

"Ah ha! ah ha! um h'm! that's exactly my opinion," said Mr. Lilburn, looking round upon them with a smile. "I have noticed many times, with sincere admiration, the admirable manner in which the children of these families are trained. I only wish I'd been favored with such examples before I went at the business myself."

"I see no reason why you should, Cousin Ronald," returned the captain, "for the only one of your offspring with whom I am acquainted, seems to me to be all a father could ask or wish."

"Ah ha! um h'm! I'll no deny that my Hugh is as fine a lad as could be found in a day's travel; and Malcolm not a whit behind him; but neither will I deny that the credit belongs more to the native goodness o' the lads than to their father's training."

It was a fine breezy morning, with a delicious
coolness in the air, and all keenly enjoyed the
walk to the beach.   They spent a few moments
there, then climbed the rocks and passed along
the summit till they reached the deep fissure
called Purgatory.   There the children, carefully guarded by their parents, lest a false step
should precipitate them into the deep chasm,
were allowed to gaze into its depths for a moment, then led away and seated on a rock to rest.

Most of the older ones lingered a little
longer, watching the movement of the water at
the bottom, and speculating about the depth
and width of the chasm, and what would be the
dire consequence of a fall into it.

"I wouldn't advise you to try it, my young
friends," said Mr. Embury.   "It must be fully
fifty feet down to the water, and if you reached
the bottom alive you wouldn't remain so many
minutes."

"No, I suppose not," said Walter, reflectively; "but the fissure is not very wide and I
think I could jump across."

"Oh, Walter, don't think of such a thing!"
exclaimed Rosie, stepping back suddenly, at
the same time catching him by the arm and
pulling him away.

"Why, Rosie, do you think I could be such
a goose as to attempt anything so foolhardy

as that, when nothing was to be gained by it?"
he exclaimed, in a tone between vexation and
amusement.

"No, I don't," she said, drawing a long
breath, "but the very thought of it frightens
me."

"To run such a risk without any good object
in view—such, for instance, as the saving of the
life of someone else—would be a very wicked
thing, I think," said Mr. Keith.

"I entirely agree with you," said Captain
Raymond, "no one has a right to rush uncalled
into the presence of his Maker.

"Oh, I shouldn't think anybody would ever
want to try jumping across here!" exclaimed
Grace. "I wonder if anyone ever did."

"It is said that the thing was done once
under peculiar circumstances," replied Mr.
Embury. "The story is that a young and
pretty girl, who had many admirers, suitors for
her hand, came here with one of them and
dared him to jump across the chasm, saying
that if he did so successfully, she would marry
him; otherwise she would not; whereupon he
attempted the dangerous feat and was successful. But his love for his cruel charmer was
gone; he turned toward her, lifted his hat,
bade her farewell, walked away and left her
never to return."

"Which served her just right," exclaimed Lucilla emphatically. "She couldn't have loved him. Why, I wouldn't let an entire stranger do so dangerous a thing, if I could hinder him. Unless it might be somebody who was here to fight against my country," she added as an afterthought, and with a little laugh.

"You would have let Prescott do it, I suppose—Prescott, the Revolutionary tyrant—had you been with him here and he had shown an inclination to try his skill in that line," said Walter.

"I think I shouldn't have made any very strong objection; for certainly many of my countrymen would have been far better off with him down there at the bottom of the fissure, than where he was—and had no business to be. Do you remember the story of the Tory lady at a ball in Philadelphia, while the British were in possession there, who, when the British general, Sir Henry Clinton, ordered the band to play, 'Britons, Strike Home,' said, 'You should say, "Britons, go home"'?"

"Yes, that was pretty good," laughed Walter. "The ladies had at least one advantage over the men in those days, they could give the invaders many a home thrust with their tongues without much danger of personal violence or imprisonment, in return for it."

"That reminds me of a little anecdote of something that occurred in Charleston, South Carolina, when they were in possession there," said Grandma Elsie. "One of the British officers had taken a great fancy to a beautiful American girl, but she would have nothing to do with him; which, of course, made him very angry. One day they met in the street. A big negro was near at hand and the British officer said to him, so that the lady could hear, 'Go and kiss that lady, and I'll give you a guinea.'

"'Yes,' said she, 'come and kiss me. I'd a thousand times rather be kissed by you than by him.' "

"So he didn't make much by that," laughed Mr. Embury.

"I wonder if the darkey did kiss her," said Grace. "I'm glad I wasn't in her place, if she had to let either him or the British officer do it."

"And you would rather be living now, wouldn't you, daughter?" said her father, giving her a loving look.

"And belong to you, papa? Yes, indeed!" she replied.

"How very straight these openings in the rocks are!" remarked Walter. "They look as if they had been cut with a knife."

"Yes, it is very strange," said Rosie.

Then perceiving that the others had turned away and were going toward the spot where the little ones were, they followed.

"There is a fine prospect here on both land and water," remarked Mr. Embury. "Do you see that hanging rock over yonder—not close to the water. That, they say, is where Bishop Berkeley used to preach. I visited it the other day, and found it so hard a place to climb to that I should think his congregations must have been small; unless they stood in the valley below; which would make his pulpit very high above them."

"Where is the house he lived in?" asked Rosie.

"At some distance, I believe. I have not seen it yet."

"Now," said Captain Raymond, "will any or all of you take a sail in the *Dolphin?* You can all see her lying out yonder and the row-boat will soon carry us to her. There is plenty of room for everyone here, a warm welcome if they choose to go aboard, and a more delightful day for a sail around the island could hardly be found."

All accepted the invitation with alacrity, descending the rocks to the beach at once, and were soon aboard.

They found it a very delightful trip. The captain, having been frequently in those waters, was able to point out every interesting object, name all the islands, and call attention to the still visible ruins of fortifications on Gold, Goat, Rose, Contour, and Canonicut islands. That last, he told them, was the Dumplings Fort, or Fort Canonicut; and directly opposite was the Castle Hill of the Revolution, now Fort Adams, three and a quarter miles below Newport. In calling attention to it, Captain Raymond remarked, "That is, as regards strength, the third fortress in the United States. It is Newport's defence against foreign foes."

"I am glad she has such a defence," said Mr. Embury. "But may she never suffer again from a foreign foe as she did in Revolutionary days. Perhaps you all remember that her population in 1774, the year before that war began, was eleven thousand, and in 1782 it was reduced to only about six thousand, and private property to the value of $624,000 in silver money had been destroyed."

"Yes," said the captain, "there had been great and wanton destruction by the ruthless invaders, in both town and country. The island of Rhode Island had been so celebrated for its beauty and salubrity, before that war,

that it was the chosen resort of the rich and
philosophical from nearly every part of the
civilized world; but war had sadly changed it
before the British left, after three years of
occupancy, in which they had pillaged and
destroyed more like savages than civilized
men; though after Prescott was superseded by
Sir Robert Pigot as commander of the British
forces on the island, the people were much
relieved. They were treated with respect, and
plunder ceased. General Pigot was a gentleman and no marauder."

CHAPTER XVII.

THE sun was setting as the *Dolphin* discharged her complement of passengers, and
they walked up the valley to their temporary
abodes. They had had their evening meal upon
the yacht, and the little ones were ready and
glad to be taken at once to their beds, the
older to sit in restful quiet upon the porches,
enjoying the evening breeze, a cheerful chat
over all they had seen and learned in their
delightful little excursion around the island,
and in laying plans for others of the same kind,
and for walks and drives here and there, till
every interesting spot in the neighborhood
should have received from them due attention.
Also in making arrangements for attending the
public service of the sanctuary on the approaching Lord's day; the captain having already
planned for the *Dolphin's* crew to do the same,
taking turns so that the vessel would not be
left at any time entirely unguarded.

When all these questions had been discussed
and settled, though it was still early, they held
their accustomed evening family service, and

retired to rest, that they might hope to awake in good season refreshed and ready to engage with enjoyment in the sacred duties of the holy day.

"It dawned a lovely autumn day, a cool refreshing breeze coming in from the bay, making the walk through the lovely valley to the open churches a pleasure as well as duty.

The services over, they returned home, and after partaking of a simple dinner, gathered upon the largest of the porches, and each one old enough to read, with Bible in hand, they spent an hour in the study of its sacred pages.

The subject engaging their attention was the way of salvation; Mr. Keith, who was the leader, called for texts showing the one true way, and they were given by one and another as they found them in God's word.

"'If thou shalt confess with thy mouth the Lord Jesus, and shalt believe in thine heart that God hath raised him from the dead, thou shalt be saved. For with the heart, man believeth unto righteousness; and with the mouth, confession is made unto salvation,'" repeated the captain, adding the comment, "Let us notice that the belief which is unto salvation is evidenced by holy living; belief that is not unto righteousness is not a true and living faith. The devils believe and tremble, but theirs is

not a saving faith, for they do not love and
trust in Jesus. It is the faith which worketh
by love that saves."

"Yes," said Mr. Dinsmore; "it is not enough
to have no doubt of the truth of the Gospel—the
good news of salvation through Jesus Christ—
but we must give ourselves to him, love him
and rejoice in his love to us."

"And oh, what a blessing that all may have
that faith who will come to Jesus for it,"
remarked Mr. Embury; "every one, old and
young. 'Look unto me and be ye saved all ye
ends of the earth.'"

"Yes," added Mr. Keith, "there are many
good and desirable things to which some of us
can never attain, but salvation by faith is within the reach of all who will come to Jesus for
it. He says, 'Him that cometh to me, I will in
no wise cast out.'"

It was Mrs. Dinsmore's turn and she repeated:
"'Without faith it is impossible to please him;
for he that cometh to God must believe that he
is, and that he is a rewarder of them that dili-
gently seek him.'"

"'Fight the good fight of faith, lay hold on
eternal life,'" repeated Mrs. Keith.

Then Mrs. Embury: "'Now the just shall live
by faith: but if any man draw back, my soul
shall have no pleasure in him. But we are not

of them that draw back unto perdition; but of them that believe to the saving of the soul.' "

"And those who believe in Jesus are not to hide their faith, as that of which they are ashamed," said Grandma Elsie; "we are to confess with the mouth, letting it be known that we believe in Christ and take him for our Saviour. His own word is, 'Whosoever shall confess me before men, him shall the Son of man also confess before the angels of God.' "

It was Evelyn's turn. "In Habakkuk ii. 4," she said, "I read, 'The just shall live by faith.' Again in Romans i. 17, 'The just shall live by faith.' Galatians iii. 11: 'But that no man is justified by the law in the sight of God, it is evident: for, The just shall live by faith.' And here,"—again turning over the leaves of her Bible,—"Hebrews x. 38, 'Now the just shall live by faith: but if any man draw back, my soul shall have no pleasure in him.' "

She paused, and Lucilla repeated the next verse, " ' But we are not of them who draw back unto perdition; but of them that believe to the saving of the soul.' "

Now it was Rosie's turn. "I will read a few verses from the third chapter of Romans," she said, and proceeded to do so. " ' Even the righteousness of God which is by faith of Jesus Christ unto all, and upon all them that believe;

for there is no difference: for all have sinned,
and come short of the glory of God; being justified freely by his grace through the redemp-
tion that is in Christ Jesus.' "

She ceased and Grace, who had turned to
the same passage, went on with the reading,
" 'Whom God hath set forth to be a propiti-
ation, through faith in his blood, to declare his
righteousness for the remission of sins that are
past, through the forbearance of God: To declare, I say, at this time his righteousness: that
he might be just, and the justifier of him which
believeth in Jesus.' " She ceased, and Walter
went on:

" 'Where is boasting then? It is excluded.
By what law? Of works? Nay; but by the
law of faith. Therefore we conclude, that a
man is justified by faith without the deeds of
the law.' "

" ' Therefore being justified by faith, we
have peace with God through our Lord Jesus
Christ,' " repeated Annis, in low, feeling tones.

Then her husband took it up: " 'What shall
we say then? That the Gentiles, which followed not after righteousness, have attained to
righteousness, even the righteousness which is
of faith. But Israel, which followed after
righteousness, hath not attained to the law
of righteousness. Wherefore? Because they

sought it not by faith, but as it were by the works of the law. For they stumbled at that stumbling stone; as it is written, Behold I lay in Sion a stumbling stone and rock of offence: and whosoever believeth on him shall not be ashamed.' "

Walter then spoke again and his was the closing text. " 'Watch ye, stand fast in the faith, quit you like men, be strong.' "

"Let us not forget," said Mr. Keith, "that we are to confess Christ, owning ourselves as his disciples, under his authority, and ready to submit to it in all things. Let us not forget that his own word is, 'If any man will be my disciple, let him deny himself, and take up his cross and follow me.' His cross, let us remember; not one of our own devising, or one laid upon us by some earthly power without the Master's word. He alone is Lord of the conscience and the Bible is his word, revealing to us his will. Also his own command to each one of us is, 'Search the Scriptures; for in them ye have eternal life: and they are they which testify of me.' We must never be afraid or ashamed to let it be known at any time, or in any company or place, that we are disciples of Christ, to whom the love of our hearts and the obedience of our lives are due."

A moment of silence followed the closing of

Mr. Keith's remarks; a silence presently broken
by Mrs. Travilla's sweet voice beginning the
hymn:

> "Jesus! and shall it ever be.
> A mortal man ashamed of Thee?"

The others joined in, filling the air with
sweet melody.

Prayers and other hymns followed till the
hour set apart for the service had more than
passed away.

CHAPTER XVIII.

THE next morning proved bright and fair, as lovely a day as one could desire; no cloud in the sky save the light fleecy ones that are not the presage of a storm. Our friends in the cottages gathered about their breakfast tables in rare good spirits, in spite of the fact that Walter was to leave them that day, by the evening boat, for his first experience of life away from home and mother.

The lad appeared in high spirits, partly real but partly only assumed, to hide the sinking of heart that at times oppressed him at the thought of so long a separation from her who had been almost all the world to him from babyhood till now, when he began to consider himself on the very verge of manhood.

She saw it if no one else did, and her tender mother heart ached for her "baby boy." For herself too, that she must do without him and his loving caresses, for months, and know that he was exposed to many a trial and temptation from which mother love could not shield him. But oh, there was comfort in the thought that

her best Friend was his also, and would still
be as near as ever to both mother and son; still
to them, as to all His children, the Hearer and
Answerer of prayer.

"Well, what is to be done to-day?" asked
Rosie, when the meal had fairly begun.

"I propose a visit to 'Tonomy Hill' for one
thing," said Captain Raymond, addressing his
remark to the company in general.

"Where is that, and what particular claim
has it upon our attention?" queried Mr. Dinsmore in return.

"It is about a mile and a half north of Newport," replied the captain. "Tonomy is an
abbreviation of Miantonomoh, the name of a
Narragansett sachem whose seat it was in early
times. It is a rocky eminence and the commanding site of a small fort or redoubt during
the Revolutionary war. It is said to be the
highest land upon the island except Quaker
Hill, which you will remember we saw toward
the northern end as we sailed round on Saturday."

"Ah, yes! where the battle was fought
between the British and our forces under Greene
and Sullivan."

"Is there anything to be seen there—on
Tonomy Hill—but the ruin of the little fortifi-
cation?" asked Rosie.

"Yes," replied the captain. "The hill is 270 feet above the bay, and from it we may obtain a fine view on all sides. On the south and west the city and harbor of Newport, and many islands in the harbor with the remains of fortifications—Canonicut, with its ruined fort, for one. Ah, I am forgetting that you saw all from the *Dolphin* the other day! Still we could not from there take in the whole view at once as we may from the hill top.

"Looking oceanward beyond the city, we can see Fort Adams; and, with a spy-glass, the dim outline of Block Island; beyond it in the Atlantic, perhaps, if your eyes are good, a faint view, a little more to the eastward, of the nearest shore of Martha's Vineyard; also of some of the islands in Buzzard's Bay.

"On the east can be seen Warren and Bristol, and the top of Mount Hope, the throne of King Philip. To the north there will be a good view of Narragansett Bay and the towns along its shores."

"Indeed, captain, you make it seem very well worth while to go there," observed Mrs. Dinsmore.

"I think that when we get there and look about and around, upon all that is to be seen, you will be still better convinced of it," returned the captain. "In addition to what I have already mentioned we can look upon a large part of the cultivated fields of this island, and find them rich in natural productions as well as in historical associations."

"Oh, let us go by all means!" exclaimed Violet. "Perhaps our little folks might not care for it, or might find the climb up the hill too fatiguing, but they can be left in the yacht or carriage, whichever the trip is made in."

"Oh, mamma!" exclaimed little Elsie, "I should very much rather go up that hill with the rest of you, if you will only let me!"

"Well, dear, I should like to let you do as you prefer, but, of course, it must be just as your papa says," replied Violet, smiling down affectionately into the eager, pleading little face.

"And papa says you may go if you wish to," said the captain, in his kind, pleasant tones.

"Me too, papa?" asked Ned eagerly.

"Yes, you too, if you wish to, son," replied his father. "I think even my baby boy will enjoy the drive, the climb up the hill, and the lovely view from its top."

"We are going to drive, are we, papa?" queried Lucilla.

"Yes; I have ordered carriages from Newport to be here by nine o'clock; so that all who wish can drive. But should anyone prefer the yacht it is at their service. Also, it will be welcome to any who desire a sail afterward."

After a little more talk, first among themselves, then along with the occupants of the other cottage, it was decided that all would take the drive to Tonomy Hill and see the view; then some would drive elsewhere, others would board the yacht and have a sail.

The engaged vehicles were already at hand, and in a few minutes the entire company of adults and children were on the way to Tonomy Hill.

All, old and young, greatly enjoyed the drive, and the captain was plied with questions about this object and that. The windmills particularly interested little Elsie and Ned. Their father explained what they were, and why there were so many of them, that they were made necessary by the absence of streams sufficiently strong to turn water-wheels, and, of one standing at the junction of the main road and the lane leading to the Hill, he remarked: "That is an old, old one, built years before the Revolutionary War. At the time of the war it and the dwelling-house near by were owned by a man named Hubbard. He was one of the many Americans whom Prescott turned out of their houses, to take shelter in barns and other miserable abiding places, while his soldiers took possession of their comfortable homes."

"What a shame!" exclaimed Ned. "Papa, I'm glad we don't have those bad fellows here now."

"So am I," replied his father. "We ought to thank God every day for making us so free, and giving us this dear land of our own. I hope my boy will always remember to do so."

Reaching the top of the hill, they found the view from it all that the captain had said. Calling attention to it, now on this side, now on that, he named the different towns and other objects worthy of particular attention. Mount Hope was one, and again he spoke of it as the former home of King Philip.

"Papa," said Elsie, "who was he? I thought we never had any king in our country."

"The Indians used to have them, and he was king of one of their tribes," was the reply.

"Is there a story about him, papa?" she asked.

"Yes. Would you like to hear it?"

"Oh, yes, sir! yes, indeed! you know I always like stories."

"Yes; even if they are rather sad; as this one is. But if you wish, I will tell you a little about it now; perhaps more at another time."

"Oh, tell it all, if you please, Brother Levis," said Rosie. "I don't believe any one of us would object to hearing it."

Several of the others joined in the request, and the captain, ever ready to oblige, began at once.

"His original name was Metacomet, but he is frequently spoken of as King Philip and also as Pometacom. His father was Massasoit, whose dominions extended from this Narragansett Bay to Massachusetts. Massasoit took two of his sons, Metacomet and Wamsutta, to Plymouth and asked that English names might be given them. His request was granted, one being called Philip and the other Alexander.

"Upon the death of the father, Alexander became chief in his stead, but soon died suddenly, of poison, it was supposed, and Philip became chief or king in his stead. He was a bright, enterprising man; sagacious, brave, and generous. He soon perceived that his people were being robbed by the whites, who took possession of the best lands, and killed off the game and the fish upon which the Indians had been used to subsist.

"Philip's tribe was known as the Wampanoags, or Pokanokets, and their principal village was there upon Mount Hope. They, and other tribes as well, felt that they had been greatly injured by the whites, and planned an offensive alliance against them.

"Philip began his war preparations by sending the women and children of the tribe away from Mount Hope to the Narragansetts for protection. Then he warned some of the whites with whom he was friendly of the coming storm, that they might seek places of safety, and, when they were gone, bade his followers swear eternal hostility to the whites.

"A dreadful war followed, beginning on the 24th of June, 1675, and lasting for more than a year. The whites suffered a great deal, but the Indians still more. Particularly the Narragansetts, who were treated with great cruelty because they had given shelter to the Wampanoags and their families.

"They had a fort on an elevation of three or four acres surrounded by a swamp, studded with brambles and thick underbrush. There were three thousand Indians in it—mostly women and children. The whites surprised them, burned their palisades and straw-covered wigwams, and the poor creatures were burned, suffocated, butchered, frozen, or drowned. Six hundred warriors and a thousand women and children were killed, and all the winter provision of the tribe destroyed. Their chief,

Canonchet, escaped then, but was captured and killed the next summer.

"It was on the 12th of the next August that a renegade Indian guided a large party of white men to the camp of the Wampanoags. The Indians were asleep, King Philip among them. After the first shot or two he woke, sprang to his feet, gun in hand, and tried to escape, but, as he stumbled and fell in the mire, was shot dead by a treacherous Indian. His death ended the war."

"Poor fellow!" sighed Grace. "He was certainly treated with great injustice and cruelty. I don't see how the whites could be so blind to the fact that the Indians had the best right to this country, and that it was wicked to rob them of their lands."

"Self-interest is apt to have a very blinding influence," said her father. "And I am afraid we must acknowledge that the whites were the first aggressors, in their grasping seizure of so much of the land of which the Indians were the original and rightful possessors."

All having now looked their fill, they returned to their carriages and drove to other points of interest, one of them Whitehall, the old residence of Bishop Berkeley. It was a place that all cared to see, especially a room in it formerly occupied by the dean, where was a fireplace, ornamented with Dutch tiles, placed there by the dean himself.

"Oh, how old they must be!" exclaimed Grace.

"Yes, not much, if at all, under two hundred years old," said Walter. "It sometimes seems odd how much longer things may last than people."

"In this world, you mean," said his grandfather; "but do not forget that man is immortal, and must live somewhere to all eternity."

"And Bishop Berkeley is no doubt spending his eternity in a far lovelier paradise than that with which he was familiar in this world," remarked Mrs. Travilla.

"Yes, indeed! 'Blessed are the dead who die in the Lord,'" quoted Evelyn softly, thinking of the dear father who had left her for the better land years ago.

CHAPTER XIX.

DINNER was ready to be put upon the table when the party reached again their temporary home, and their long drive had given each one an appetite that made the meal most enjoyable. They rested upon the porches for a short time after leaving the table, then set out for a walk to the beach, Walter at his mother's side, Violet, the captain, and their two little ones near at hand. These were at some distance in the rear of the young girls, who had started for the beach a few minutes earlier.

"Mother," said Walter, "I should like very much to see that dear old lady Cousin Molly talks about; also the old Revolutionary house she lives in. Do you think we might call there without seeming to intrude?"

"Really I do not know," replied Mrs. Travilla. "If Molly were only here she could judge better than I."

"Perhaps she is there," suggested Walter. "I noticed that she started a little ahead of the girls."

"So she did," said Violet, overhearing their

252

talk, "and I think she is probably there now, for she was telling me last evening that she felt anxious that you, Walter, should see her dear old lady before leaving to-night. Ah! and yonder they both are at the gate of the house now."

"Then I would suggest that you three hasten on, leaving me to follow more slowly with the children. It would hardly do to overwhelm the old lady with so large a company at once," said the captain, and they promptly carried out his suggestion. Mrs. Barker and Molly were standing by the front gate chatting as they came up.

"Ah, here they are, Mrs. Barker!" said Molly; "my cousins, Mrs. Travilla, her daughter, Mrs. Raymond, and her son Walter. He is the lad I was telling you of, who starts for college to-night, and was very desirous to see you and your revolutionary house before going."

"And to hear all you can tell me about its experiences in those days, Mrs. Barker, if you will be so kind," added Walter, with a polite bow and his most insinuating smile.

"I shall be happy to tell and show all I can to you and your mother and sister," replied the old lady, leading the way toward the house, her guests following.

She took them over the greater part of it, telling them what rooms had been occupied by the Hessians, and what by the family while the unwelcome intruders were there. They were much interested in all she told them, and admired her housekeeping, everything being in beautiful order. She told them the Mr. Barker of those days was a true patriot, in fact, a spy working for the American cause, and when their call was finished and they were taking their departure, she went with them to the gate, and pointing out a ledge of rock on the farther side of the valley, beyond the cottages they were occupying, told them that in revolutionary times that was a part of the large tract of land owned by Isaac Barker; that, in those days, instead of the stone wall now running along its edge overlooking the water, there was a rail fence; and that Isaac Barker was in the habit of signalling the patriot troops encamped on an island opposite, whenever there was an important item of news for them, and that he did so by alterations in the fence, made under his supervision by the unsuspecting Hessians."

"Oh, that was good!" cried Walter; "but did the British never catch him at it?"

"No, never," she replied. "If they had, his life would not have been worth much."

"You must think a great deal of this old house," said Walter, turning and looking it over with admiring eyes. "If it were mine I wouldn't give it for any of the grand palaces built in these later days."

"Nor would I," she said. "Come and see it again; it and me; if you care to do so."

"Thank you; I should enjoy doing so, but I leave to-night for college."

"Ah? I am glad for you; for a good education is worth more than money or almost any other earthly thing."

"So I think, because it will enable me, or anyone who has it, to be more useful in the world."

"That is a right feeling," she said; then turning to the ladies gave them a warm invitation to call again any day, as they passed on their way to the beach.

"Thank you, Mrs. Barker," said Grandma Elsie. "It is quite likely we may do so, for we have greatly enjoyed our chat with you."

"And will be glad to have you return our call, if you can conveniently do so, while we linger in your neighborhood," added Violet.

Arrived at the beach, Violet joined her husband and the young folks there, but her mother and Walter passed on up the cliff, the lad saying laughingly that he wanted another peep into Purgatory before leaving the neighborhood; but, as his mother well understood, a bit of private chat with her was the chief object he had in view.

They took a peep into the chasm, then wandered away a little and sat down side by side upon a ledge of rock. Looking at him with her own loving smile, she laid her hand in his. He clasped it tightly, while unbidden tears sprang to his eyes.

"Mother," he said low and tremulously, "my own dear mother! You are almost all the world to me. I think no other fellow had so dear and sweet a mother as mine. I don't know how I shall ever stand it to pass weeks and months without a sight of your dear face."

"Ah, you will soon learn to do without me," she said, between a sigh and a smile. "But I do not believe my dear baby boy will ever cease to love his mother, or to try to make her happy by a faithful attendance to all his duties. But oh, above all, try to please and honor the God of your fathers whose servant you profess to be. Begin every day with an earnest supplication for strength to perform every duty and resist every temptation."

"It is my fixed purpose to do so, mother dear, and I know you will be ever helping me with your prayers," he answered earnestly.

"Oh, what a blessing it is to have a praying, Christian mother! And I know that you will write to me often, and that your dear letters will be a great help to me in my efforts to resist temptation and keep in the strait and narrow path."

"I hope so," she said; "also that my dear youngest son will never learn to conceal things from his mother, but will write me freely of all that concerns him, never doubting my love or my interest in it all, for his dear sake."

"Doubt your dear love, mother? No, never for one moment! Oh, it will be hard to part from you to-day, even though I hope to see you again before you go home!"

"Yes, I expect to give you a call at the college, to see that my dear son is made as comfortable as possible, and to take a view of his room and all his surroundings, that I may be able to picture him in my mind's eye at his studies, recitations, and sports."

"Just as I can see my loved mother in every room of the dear home at Ion, or the other one at Viamede, should you go there at any time without me," he returned, making a determined effort to speak lightly. "It seems a little hard to start off without you, mother; but as Cousin Cyril has kindly promised to go with me, I shall do very well, especially with the knowledge that I am to see you again in a few days."

"Yes," she said, "and you will like those New Jersey relatives of his, who are more distantly related to us, when you become acquainted with them, as I hope you will at some not very distant day."

"The uncle he is expecting to visit there is a brother of Cousin Annis, is he not?" asked Walter.

"Yes."

"Then I should think she and her husband, Cousin Ronald, would go with Cousin Cyril."

"I think they will follow a few days hence, when we start for home," she answered.

Just at that moment they were startled by a wild shriek, as of one in great peril or affright, instantly followed by a sound as of a heavy body plunging into the water. Both started to their feet, Walter exclaiming, "Oh, mother! someone must have fallen into that dreadful deep chasm they call Purgatory! Oh, what can we do?"

"Nothing," she answered, with a laugh that sounded slightly hysterical. "See! Cousin Ronald and several of the others have come up the hill unnoticed by us."

"Oh! I think it was rather too bad for him

to startle you so, mamma dear!" exclaimed Walter.

"Yes, I must acknowledge that it was," returned Mr. Lilburn, who had now drawn near enough to overhear the remark. "Pardon me, Cousin Elsie; I really did not intend to give you such a fright; for I deemed it likely you would know at once that it was I and none other."

"As I probably should, had I been aware of your vicinity," she returned, in a pleasant tone; "but my boy and I were so engrossed with our talk that we did not perceive your approach. I think Walter and I must now go back to the cottage and see to the packing of his trunk."

"Cannot I do that, mamma?" queried Violet.

"Thank you, daughter, I have no doubt you could, but I have a fancy for the job myself," was the pleasant-toned reply. "Besides, your place is with your husband and little ones, who, I think, would find it agreeable and beneficial to remain here on the beach for another hour or so."

"I haven't unpacked much since we came here, mother," remarked Walter, as they walked away together, "so that it will not be a long job to get my things in my trunk, but I am glad you came away so early with me, as it gives us time and opportunity for another private chat."

"Yes, my dear boy, that was my principal object in proposing this early return, but I hope for many another pleasant chat with my dear youngest son in the years to come," his mother responded cheerfully.

"I haven't seen quite all the places in and about Newport or Middletown that I should take an interest in examining," remarked Walter. "But I presume I may hope to come again some day?"

"Oh, yes; possibly a good many times in the course of a few years; though there are many other places in our great, beautiful country that are quite as well worth visiting, and far better worth seeing than some noted resorts in Europe. I want my sons and daughters to appreciate their own country," she went on, her sweet face lighting with enthusiasm, "with all that is beautiful and valuable in it, as well as its free institutions—religious, civil, and political."

"I think I do, mamma," he said, with a smile. "You have brought up all your children to admire and love their own land, believing it the best and greatest country in all the wide world."

"Yes, and yet, alas! there is a vast deal of wickedness in it," she sighed; "wickedness, error, superstition, and vice, which we should make it our life work to try to root out."

"As I truly intend to, mamma. But are not most of the ignorant and vicious those who have come in from foreign lands?"

"A very great many—a very large majority no doubt are," she answered; "and yet there are many ignorant and vicious ones who are native born; not a few of them being the children of natives. Some of the Tories of revolutionary times were even worse than savages. 'The heart is deceitful above all things and desperately wicked,' applies to the whole of Adam's fallen race, and each one of us needs to pray, 'Create in me a clean heart, O God; and renew a right spirit within me.' "

"I feel that I do, mother, but you have always seemed to me so perfect that it is difficult to realize that it can be so with you," said the lad, turning upon her eyes filled with ardent love and admiration.

"That is doubtless because your eyes are blinded by filial love, my dear boy," she returned, with her sweet and loving smile.

They presently reached the house, and Walter set about his packing, under his mother's supervision, which made the work seem but a pleasant pastime. It did not take long and, seated together in one of the porches, they had time before the return of the others for a confidential chat, such as Walter dearly loved to have with his mother.

Then came the call to supper, and the meal was scarcely over when the hack was announced as at the door; there were hasty leave-takings, his mother's the last for Walter. She strained him to her heart with some whispered words of love, while he embraced her with ardent affection, and in a moment more he was in the hack, with Mr. Keith by his side, and they were driving rapidly away toward the city to take the night train for New York.

CHAPTER XX.

The shades of evening had begun to fall. A cool breeze made the brightly lighted parlor more attractive than the porches, and there the older ones gathered, while the mothers saw their weary little ones to bed. The gentlemen had their newspapers, Mrs. Dinsmore and Mrs. Travilla their fancy work, while the four young girls, in a group by themselves, chatted and laughed together, discussing the sights and scenes through which they had passed that day, and the bits of history connected with them.

The captain presently threw aside his paper, and taking a vacant seat on the sofa beside his daughter Grace, asked in tender tones, as he passed an arm about her and drew her close, if she felt very weary from the day's exertions.

"Not so very, papa dear," she answered, laying her head on his shoulder and smiling up into the eyes bent so lovingly upon her. "I think I never had a better time. Have we been to all the places of interest now?"

"Not quite all," he replied; "there are a

few others to which we may take pleasant little jaunts in the week or so we expect to tarry here."

"Vaucluse for one, I should say," remarked Mr. Embury, laying aside his paper and joining in the talk.

"Where is that?" asked Mrs. Dinsmore.

"Over on the shore of the eastern bay, and about six miles out from Newport. It is a noted country seat, at present unoccupied except in small part by a caretaker and his wife. It has a very neglected look, but is still well worth seeing, I have been told. But here comes my Molly with a manuscript in her hand. Something to read to us, I suppose. Is it, my dear?"

"Yes," she said, with a smile; "provided you all wish to hear it. A story of the ship *Palatine* from Holland, which struck on Sandy Point of this island early in the last century. I have used the facts as far as they could be obtained, and drawn upon my imagination for the rest. If all would like to hear it, I shall be glad to have your opinions and criticisms before offering it for publication."

"Suppose you put it to vote, my dear," suggested her husband. "We are all here now except the little folks, who have gone to their beds," he added; glancing at Isadore and Violet,

who had come into the room just in time to
hear Molly's last sentence.

"I shall be glad to heard it, Molly. I always
have enjoyed such of 'your productions as have
come under my notice," said Violet, in a lively
tone, as she took the seat her husband had hastened to offer.

"And I can echo those sentiments," added
Isadore lightly, taking possession of an easy
chair gallantly drawn forward for her by her
Uncle Dinsmore.

Thus encouraged, Mrs. Embury began at
once.

"Story of the ship *Palatine*," she read.

"Some time in the early years of the last
century, a ship named the *Palatine* left Holland for America, bearing a large number of
emigrants, whose destination was the then
colony of Pennsylvania, where they intended
to buy land and settle; and for that reason
they were carrying with them all their earthly
possessions—clothing, furniture, and money;
of which some had a good deal, others only
a little.

"Among the wealthier ones was Herr
Adolphus Follen, with his wife Margaret, his
daughters Katrina and Gretchen, and his son
Karl. Also they had with them an elderly
woman, Lisa Kuntz, who had lived with the

Follens ever since their marriage, and acted as nurse to each of their children in turn. She had no near kin, and being much attached to the family in which she had made her home for so many years, had decided to accompany them to the new world in spite of her fears of Indians and wild animals.

"As the good ship *Palatine* sailed slowly out of port, all these, with many of their fellow-passengers, stood upon her deck gazing sadly, and not a few with flowing tears, upon the fast-receding shores of their native land. Ah, how much bitterer would have been their grief, could they have foreseen the sufferings that fateful voyage held in store for them! Though they little suspected it at the time, they had fallen into the hands of men so full of the love of money, so ready to do the most dastardly deeds in order to secure it, that they were no better than the worst of cut-throats and murderers.

"The emigrants had not brought a store of provisions for the voyage, because, according to the agreement, these were to be purchased of the captain and his officers. But scarcely had they cleared the coast and stood well out to sea when they were struck with astonishment and dismay at the enormous sums asked for the merest necessaries of life: 20 guilders for a cup of water, 50 rix dollars for a ship's biscuit."

"Astounding rascality!" exclaimed Mr. Embury, as his wife paused for an instant in her reading.

"Why, how much are those coins worth in our money?" she asked. "I really do not know exactly."

"A guilder," he replied, "equals 40 cents of our money; so that 20 guilders would be $8. Think of that as the price of a cup of water! probably not the coolest or cleanest either. Then the 50 rix dollars for a ship biscuit would equal $18.25. Think of such a conspiracy as that on the part of a ship's officers to rob defenceless passengers!"

"Why, it was just dreadful!" she exclaimed. "Those officers were no better than pirates."

"Not a whit! In fact, they were pirates. But go on, my dear; let us have the rest of your story."

Mrs. Embury resumed her reading.

"'What shall we, what can we do,' asked Frau Follen of her husband. 'I fear there will be no money left for buying land when we reach America.'

"'Alas! I fear not, indeed!' he returned; 'and should anything happen to delay the vessel we may be reduced to great extremity even before reaching the shores of America. Ah, would we had been satisfied to remain in the fatherland!' he groaned in anguish of spirit.

" 'Ah, father,' said Gretchen, the eldest daughter, 'let not your heart fail you yet. Help may yet come from some unexpected quarter, and if not—if we die for lack of food— we may hope to awake from the sleep of death in the better land, to suffer and die no more. Let us trust in God and not be afraid.'

" 'You are right, my daughter,' he returned with emotion. 'But oh, God grant I may not be called to see my wife and children suffer and die for lack of food!'

"A young man standing near, one with whom they were slightly acquainted, here joined in the conversation.

" 'It is dreadful, dreadful!' he exclaimed, but speaking in a subdued tone for fear of being overheard by their inhuman oppressors, 'the way these mercenary wretches are robbing the helpless poor whom they have entrapped into their net. Every fellow of them deserves the headsman's axe, and I hope will reach it at last. Think of the exorbitant sums they are asking for the barest necessaries of life! Nor do I believe they will ever carry us to our destination, lest complaint be made of them and they be brought to condign punishment by the authorities of the land.'

" 'But, what then do you think they will do, Herr Ernesti?' asked Frau Follen, gasping with fear and horror, as she spoke.

" 'I cannot tell,' he answered. 'Mayhap land us on some desert island, and leave us there to struggle as we can for life. But, thank God, they cannot take us to any spot where He does not rule and reign, or where His ear will be deaf to the cries of His perishing ones. So, my friends, let us not give up to utter despair. "The Lord is my light and my salvation; whom shall I fear? The Lord is the strength of my life; of whom shall I be afraid?" '

" 'Yes, yes; what consolation in knowing that!' cried Gretchen, tears of mingled joy and sorrow streaming down her face. 'Father, mother, sister, and brother, we are all His and He will care for us in His own time and way.'

" But who shall describe the scenes that followed through weeks of deepest distress and agony, as fathers and mothers, husbands and wives, brothers and sisters saw their dear ones perishing with famine, while they themselves were goaded almost to madness by the pangs of hunger added to their bitter grief?

" But they were entirely in the power of their inhuman torturers, who never relaxed in their demands until they had wrenched from

their wretched victims every stiver in their
possession.

"That accomplished, and no food remaining
—unless a very, very scanty store—they,
officers and sailors, deserted the vessel, going
off in the boats, leaving their helpless victims
to their fate, for not one of them had either
the needed knowledge or strength for the man-
agement of the ship; and so she drifted aim-
lessly hither and thither at the mercy of the
winds and waves, carrying her fearful cargo of
dead and dying whither they knew not.

"To the survivors that voyage seemed like
one long, dreadful dream, full of horrors and
keenest anguish of body and mind. Of the
many emigrants who, filled with the hope of
reaching a land of freedom and plenty, had
crowded the vessel at the beginning of the
voyage, but seventeen feeble, emaciated, almost
dying creatures were left when, one cold winter
morning, about Christmas time, the now dismasted hulk of the good ship *Palatine* drifted
into Narragansett Bay and struck on Sandy
Point, Rhode Island.

"It was Sunday morning, but the good people
of the island seeing the wreck, and knowing
there might be in her some living soul in distress, hastened on board, where they found the
poor, perishing creatures, and at once carried

them all ashore save one woman—Lisa Kuntz, the nurse of the Follens, who obstinately refused to leave the vessel. She was seated upon the deck with her belongings about her, and there she was determined to stay. But she was not safe there, as the islanders well knew; for the dismasted hulk could not be secured against drifting away, and as the tide arose around it they, as a last resort, set it on fire, thinking the lone woman would certainly be frightened, and prefer coming ashore to remaining upon the burning ship. But she would not, and as the tide rose the blazing hulk drifted away, carrying her with it."

"Oh, how dreadful!" sighed several of Molly's hearers.

"Wasn't it?" she responded. "I suppose the sufferings of the poor creature must have made her insane."

"But the sixteen who were brought ashore, did they live?" asked Lucilla; and in reply Mrs. Embury resumed her reading.

"The sixteen who had been carried ashore were treated with the greatest kindness by the islanders, all their wants carefully attended to; but for nearly all of them help had come too late, and all but three soon died. Of the Follen family Gretchen alone remained, a lonely, almost heart-broken creature, having seen

father, mother, brother, and sister laid in the
grave soon after landing upon the island.   But
Herr Hubert Ernesti remained. He had been
beside her all these dreadful weeks and months,
had sympathized in all her griefs, all her sufferings of mind and body, and each had learned
to look upon the other as the nearest and dearest of all earthly beings; so that when, beside
the newly filled grave that held the last of her
family, he asked her to give herself to him
that they might meet all coming trials and
share all joys together, she did not say him
nay, or withdraw the hand he had taken in his
and held in a clasp so loving and tender.

"It was from them the islanders learned the
sad story of the terrible scenes and sufferings
on board the *Palatine;* an experience poor
Gretchen could never recall without tears.

"Hubert and she remained upon that hospitable island for some years, then left it for
their original destination, where, we will hope,
they lived out the remainder of their lives in
peace and happiness."

"And that is the end of your sad little story,
is it?" asked Rosie, as her cousin paused in
the reading.

"Of the story of those two," said Molly;
"but I have something more to read, if no one
is tired of listening."

No one seemed to be, and she resumed:

"Ever since the burning *Palatine* drifted away that night a strange light has been seen at intervals along this coast whence she departed on that last voyage. Many have seen it, and the superstitious and ignorant have looked upon it as the phantom of the burning ship *Palatine*, ever drifting upon the open sea, always burning but never consumed; seen only at long intervals, as she drifts off the western coast.

"A well-known physician of Block Island, having had two opportunities of seeing it, says, 'This curious irradiation rises from the ocean near the northern point of the island; looks like a blaze of fire; either touches the water or hovers over it. It bears no more resemblance to the *ignis fatuus* than to the aurora borealis. Sometimes it is small, resembling the light through a distant window; at others expanding to the height of a ship with all her canvas spread; the streams, somewhat blended together at the bottom, separate and distinct at the top, the middle one rising higher than the others. It is very variable—sometimes almost disappearing, then shining out anew. It changes about every three minutes; does not always return to the same place, but is sometimes seen shining at a considerable distance from the place of disappearance. It seems to have no certain line of direction. The flame, when most expanded, waves like a torch; is sometimes stationary, at others progressive. It is seen at all seasons of the year and, for the most part, in calm weather which precedes an easterly or southerly storm. It has, however, been noticed in a severe northwesterly gale and when no storm followed immediately. Its stay is sometimes short, at others all night, and it has been known to appear several nights in succession.'

" ' This light,' says another person, ' is often seen blazing at six or seven miles distance, and strangers suppose it to be a vessel on fire. The blaze emits luminous rays. A gentleman whose house is situated near the sea tells me that he has known it to illuminate considerably the walls of his room through the window; but that happens only when the light is within a half mile of the shore.' "

"But where did you learn all this, Molly?" asked her husband, as she paused to turn a leaf in her manuscript.

"From Mr. Baylor's ' History of Newport County,' lent me by my kind friend, Mrs. Barker, of the old revolutionary house," Mrs. Embury answered, then continued her reading.

"Says Mr. Joseph P. Hazard of Narragansett Pier: 'I first saw it three miles off the coast. I suspected nothing but ordinary sails until I noticed the light, upon reappearing, was apparently stationary for a few moments, when it suddenly started toward the coast, and, immediately expanding, became much less bright, assuming somewhat the form of a long, narrow jib, sometimes two of them, as if each on a different mast. I saw neither spar nor hull, but noticed that the speed was very great, certainly not less than fifteen knots, and they surged and pitched as though madly rushing upon raging billows.'"

"Superstition, every bit of it!" remarked Mr. Dinsmore, as Mrs. Embury folded her manuscript and laid it aside.

"Why this any more than the *ignis fatuus?*" queried Mr. Embury, in a tone that seemed a mixture of jest and earnestness. "Neither has as yet been altogether satisfactorily accounted for. The latter having puzzled philosophers from the time of Aristotle."

"True," said Mr. Dinsmore, "there are various theories advanced in regard to that. All we know certainly is that it is a luminous appearance frequently seen in marshy places, churchyards, and over stagnant pools."

"Has it ever been seen in this country, grandpa?" asked Grace.

"I think not," he replied, "but it is not unfrequent in the lowlands of Scotland, the south and northwest of England, or the northern parts of Germany. The time of year for its appearance is from the middle of autumn till the beginning of November."

"I think I have read that the people of the districts where it was frequently seen used to be superstitious about it in olden times; and that they called it Will-o'-the-wisp, and Jack-a-lantern."

"Yes; and believed it to be due to the agency of evil spirits who were trying to lure travellers to their destruction. And unfortunately it was sometimes mistaken by unwary travellers for a light, and in trying to reach it, thinking it shone from some human habitation where they might find shelter and a night's lodging, they would follow it and so get into, and sink in, the marsh, thus losing their lives."

"Is it not about time we were seeking our night's lodgings?" asked Mrs. Dinsmore pleasantly, as her husband concluded his sentence. "See, the clock is on the stroke of nine, which is a late enough hour for most of us now, when we are moving about so much during the day. Surely it is for Gracie, whose eyes, I notice, begin to droop."

"I think you are right, my dear," replied her husband. Then he requested Mr. Lilburn to lead their family worship.

CHAPTER XXI.

A FEW days longer our friends lingered in their pleasant cottages on the beautiful island, loath to leave it, with any one of its many interesting localities unexplored. They walked, rode, drove, and sailed about the bay, visiting now one island, and now another. Captain Raymond's acquaintance with naval and military officers, and his high reputation among them making it easy for them to gain access to vessels, forts, and fortifications.

Goat Island interested them as the place where the English ship *Liberty* was destroyed before the Revolution. They saw the noble stone pier, hundreds of feet long, visited the torpedo station, and the captain pointed out to the others the curving point on which, more than a century ago, very many pirates had been hanged.

They visited the city too, and looked with interest upon the old houses that had stood here in and before Revolutionary times; among them Redwood Library, and old Trinity Church, in which Bishop Berkeley had often preached.

The young people were much interested too,

in the old stone mill—that singular relic of the
past about which there has been so much spec-
ulation—and, when visiting the island ceme-
tery, in the plain obelisk marking the last resting place of Commodore Perry, the hero of the
battle of Lake Erie.

Many of these things the captain and his
family had seen on former visits to Newport,
yet they enjoyed seeing them again in company with those of the party to whom they
were entirely new.

But holidays must come to an end, and at
length all felt so great a drawing toward their
distant homes that a proposal to return to them
was made by Mrs. Dinsmore, and hailed with
delight by all the others.

The needed preparations were speedily made,
and early one morning they set sail in the yacht,
which before night had landed all but the captain's immediate family and Evelyn Leland in
New York, where they took a train for Philadelphia.

Mr. Cyril Keith was to meet his wife and
family there, and they, with the Emburys, were
to hasten on to their homes in Louisiana, paus-
ing on the route for only a short visit to the
neighborhood of the old home of Isadore and
Molly, and the relatives there.

Mr. and Mrs. Dinsmore had planned a short

visit to their relatives in and near Philadelphia; and his daughter Elsie, with her daughter Rosie, one to her son Walter at Princeton; while Mr. and Mrs. Lilburn were to do likewise by her brother, Donald Keith and his family, Annis feeling very happy in the thought of seeing them all, and showing them the dear, kindly old gentleman to whom she had given her heart and hand.

Having landed these passengers, the yacht changed her course, and sailed on down the Atlantic coast. The little ones were in their berths, the others all on deck.

"Now, if I were not here, you would be just a family party," remarked Evelyn, breaking a momentary silence.

"I think we are as it is," said the captain. "As you are a pupil of mine, will you not let me count you as one of my family?"

"Indeed, sir; I should be only too glad to have you do so," she answered, in a sprightly tone; "but I doubt if Lu would be willing to share her choicest treasure—her father's love— with me."

"Why, yes, I should, Eva! because he wouldn't love me any the less for loving you also," said Lulu.

"Oh, then you may adopt me just as soon as you like, captain," laughed Evelyn.

"Now, I think I have a right to some say in this matter," said Violet, in a light, jesting tone. "I object to becoming mother to a girl of your age and attainments, but am perfectly willing to have you for a sister."

"Very well, my dear, that settles it," said the captain. "You and I, Eva, will consider ourselves brother and sister."

"Ah, I like that," said Grace; "though I am not sure that I shall consider Eva my aunt. Papa, are we going directly home now?"

"Do you not see that we are hurrying onward in that direction?" he asked in reply.

A sudden thought seemed to strike Grace. "Oh, is Max in Annapolis now?" she asked.

"Yes," her father answered, with a joyous smile, "and I want to see my boy so badly that I have decided to call there for a few hours before going home; unless some of you strongly object," he added, in a jesting tone.

"Of course we do, papa," laughed Lucilla. "How can you suppose that any of us would be willing to see Max?"

"Very well, anyone who is averse to seeing him will have the privilege of shutting herself into her stateroom while he is on board, and indeed, during the whole visit to Annapolis," replied the captain.

"And I well know Lu will not be one of them," laughed Violet.

They had a speedy and pleasant voyage, a delightful little visit with Max, after that a joyful return home, followed a few weeks later by the coming of the Dinsmores, Travillas, and Lilburns, for whom some pleasant family parties were held, after which all settled down for the winter's duties and pleasures.

The captain continued to act as tutor to Evelyn and his daughters, but Rosie had forsaken the schoolroom, Walter was no longer there, and for a time it seemed a trifle lonely to the remaining ones. They soon, however, became accustomed to the state of affairs, and so deeply interested in their studies that the hours devoted to them passed very swiftly and pleasantly.

They also resumed their labors for the poor and ignorant of the neighborhood, making clothing for them, and teaching the women and girls to sew for themselves and their families, at the same time cultivating their minds and hearts to some extent, by taking turns in reading aloud to them simple and instructive tales of value for this life and the next.

It was Grandma Elsie who selected the reading matter and took the care and oversight of all the charitable work of her young friends—

directing, encouraging, and urging them on, by both precept and example.

How dearly they loved her! It might be truly said of her, as of the virtuous woman described in the last chapter of Proverbs: "She openeth her mouth with wisdom; and in her tongue is the law of kindness."

If you are interested in continuing in the
Elsie Dinsmore Collection,
Book 22
or desire a catalog of other

Sovereign Grace Publishers, Inc.
P.O. Box 4998
Lafayette, IN 47903
Phone: (765) 429-4122
Fax: (765) 429-4142

FAMILY LINEAGE

HORACE
HORACE DINSMORE SR.
HORACE DINSMORE JR. (ELSIE'S FATHER)
HORACE HOWARD (NEPHEW)

ELSIE
ELSIE GRAYSON DINSMORE
ELSIE DINSMORE TRAVILLA (ELSIE'S DAUGHTER)
ELSIE TRAVILLA (DAUGHTER OF E.D.T.)

ROSE
ROSE ALLISON DINSMORE
ROSE DINSMORE (DAUGHTER)
ROSE TRAVILLA (GRANDDAUGHTER TO R.A.D.)
ROSE HOWARD (NIECE TO R.A.D.)

EDWARD
EDWARN TRAVILLA SR.
EDWARD TRAVILLA JR. (EDDIE)
EDWARD HOWARD SR.
EDWARD HOWARD JR. (NED)
EDWARD ALLISON

ARTHUR
ARTHUR DINSMORE
ARTHUR HOWARD (NEPHEW)

FAMILY LINEAGE

WALTER
WALTER DINSMORE
WALTER CONLEY (NEPHEW)
WALTER HOWARD (NEPHEW)
WALTER TRAVILLA (GRAND NEPHEW)

HERBERT
HERBERT CARRINGTON
HERBERT CARRINGTON (NEPHEW)
HERBERT TRAVILLA (NAMESAKE)

HAROLD (HARRY)
HAROLD ALLISON
HARROLD CARRINGTON SR.
HAROLD CARRINGTON JR. (HARRY)
HAROLD TRAVILLA (NAMESAKE H.A.)
HARRY DUNCAN

ARCHIE
ARCHIE CARRINGTON
ARCHIE ROSS (NEPHEW)

SOPHIE
SOPHIE ALLISON CARRINGTON
SOPHIE ROSS (NIECE)

DAISY
DAISY ALLISON
DAISY CARRINGTON (NIECE)

www.ingramcontent.com/pod-product-compliance
Lightning Source LLC
Chambersburg PA
CBHW060007100426
42740CB00010B/1426